OTHER BOOKS BY BARBARA MOON

Joy-Filled Relationships

Handbook to Joy-Filled Parenting

Workbook for Handbook to Joy-Filled Parenting

Re-Framing Your Hurts: Why You Don't Have to Fear Emotional Pain

Living Lessons on Intimacy with Christ

Leader's Guide to Hinds' Feet on High Places,

Workbook for Hinds' Feet

Leader's Guide for The Rest of the Gospel

Workbook for the Rest of the Gospel

Jewels for My Journey

Jesus Never Fails

The Craziosity Twins

Fiction Trilogy—*The Lost Dome of Atron, The Genesis of Atron, The Redemption of Atron,*

JOY-FILLED PARENTING WITH TEENS

Hopeful Stories for Successful Relationships

by

Barbara Moon

Revised January 2018

TABLE OF CONTENTS

DEDICATION: I dedicate this book to Shawnda and Trey, Lisa and John, and Kayli. Without them it would not be the same.

THANKS: First I have to thank Dr. Jim Wilder without whom I would not know much of anything about joy-filled relationships, brain science, and Immanuel prayer. Knowing Dr. Wilder has changed my life completely. I also want to thank my awesome editor, Debbie Sellmann of *dswebdesignplus.com*. She pokes and prods and suggests until my books are so much better. And I thank my son, Bob Moon, who encourages me and does the formatting and prep for publishing.

I want to acknowledge that the some of the material here is from various writers at Life Model Works, Thrive conferences, Dr. Karl Lehman, and Ed Khouri of Equipping Hearts. If I fail to give credit, I beg grace, as so much of what I have learned has been from Dr. Wilder directly. Throughout the book and at the end I will show these other sources that readers can find online.

COVER PHOTO by Joshua Moon, my grandson.

INTRODUCTION

Parenting teens can be very different from parenting elementary children. Big changes occur; parenting often becomes more difficult. For this reason, it has become apparent to me that we need to take a serious look at this stage of life. I shall approach this look from a Christian perspective because it takes some strong faith in God's goodness for parents to work through the issues necessary to make changes and "let go" of their teens and young adults. I have noticed that the more conscientious Christian parents are the more fear they have of letting go. They are so focused on behavior, or lack thereof, that they clutch tightly and try to control every aspect of their teen's life. God designed us to individuate and become our own person, to make our own mistakes and learn from them so that the beliefs our parents tried to instill will become our own. That cannot happen unless there is room to explore, try, fail, and find grace, because allowing individuation must be done relationally.

Parents need great courage to let go and trust God while they watch their precious child become an adult. My prayer is that some of the information and stories in this book will help parents walk that journey. It won't be easy and everyone will need grace, strong support, and joy-filled community. Along the way, we will meet some real-life parents who have practiced both parenting changes and letting go as they learned and applied the relational skills that we will look at here.

I send my deepest thanks to E. John Wilder, PhD. of Life Model Works. Jim has been my mentor since 1993 and nearly all of what I will share here about relational skills I've learned from him. I give credit to him and others at Life Model for developing the practical sides of this material. I will note other resources by people from Life Model throughout the book.

Join us as we explore *Joy-Filled Parenting with Teens*. My hope is to keep this information as clear and as short as possible, but I will have to touch on several topics in order for readers to understand the real-life stories and their applications. I pray that the information will be turned into life-changing transformation for both parents and teens.

CHAPTER ONE: PARENTS OF TEENS NEED A JOY-FILLED COMMUNITY

I want to tell you a story. In fact I want to tell you lots of stories about how learning to parent through joy-filled relational skills[1] can change us and those around us. I want to begin with two moms, Lisa and Shawnda. I have seldom seen anyone's life turn around as fast as theirs did. There are many factors involved in their journeys, but the relational skills that we will look at here in this book are proving to be significant as both moms, and their husbands, apply the skills with their teens.

Notice that I included husbands here. Two moms changed how they relate and two husbands noticed and wanted to learn why. There is much to say about having both parents working together. But if that is not how it works for all of us, God can accomplish much growth when just one parent changes. As we read, examples from Lisa, Shawnda, and other parents will be scattered throughout the book, making the relational skills come alive with practicality. So let's look briefly at Lisa's and Shawnda's journeys separately. What were they like before learning about relational joy and how the brain works in relationships? What changed in their parenting styles? With which one do you most identify? Their journeys will bring us hope. (Some story tellers have requested that their names be changed.)

Lisa

To answer the question about how Lisa's parenting style changed, let's hear it in her own words:

> *My husband, John, and I have 15 and 18 year old sons—Jonathan and Jason. Our goal has been that our kids will become successful, emotionally healthy adults.*
>
> *Our focus was on making our sons responsible and helping them reach their potential by giving them consequences for*

---

[1] There are 19 relational skills. For details see *Transforming Fellowship*, Chris M. Coursey, lifemodelworks.org

their bad choices, but doing that with "love and empathy." The problem is I had a blind spot. I didn't know what true love and empathy really were. In fact, I didn't even have love and empathy to give my kids due to my own dysfunctional childhood.

So as I focused on giving consequences for their behavior, my relationship with them continued to deteriorate further and further. They were withdrawn, depressed, and angry. There was constant sibling rivalry. It seemed they truly hated each other. They never looked at me or my husband and we coexisted in our lonely house together. We were constantly arguing and having daily power struggles as I tried to make them do what I thought would make them into successful adults. There was no joy in our home; no one was glad to be together.

Then I started going to a class called Joy-Filled Relationships. In that class I started realizing that my focus on controlling their behavior had hurt my sons and my relationship with them. I discovered that I did not have a strong loving secure bond with them. The reason they were fighting all the time was because there was not enough love in our home to go around. So they were fighting to get what they could through negative attention.

I began learning that if I want joy-filled relationships with my kids, I need to make my relationship with them more important than the problem. So, their hearts needed to become more important to me than their success as future adults.

Within a very short time of attending the JFR class, I began getting the healing and building the maturity in my own life so that I could give my sons what they needed to heal and start maturing as well. I began seeing results quickly with my then 17 year old son. (We will call him Jason.) One day I could sense we were starting down that old path of power struggle and I zipped my mouth. He stormed out to the garage and I took some time to get the relational circuits of my brain back on, as I had learned in our class. With a softer heart, I went to him, knelt beside him, and waited for him to look at me. I used my new skills of synchronizing with him without words, only my eyes. I could literally see the hardness in him start to melt away. I reached out and gave him an appropriate gentle touch on his back and then walked inside. By the time he returned to the family room, he was joyful and had a bounce in his step. His eyes were filled with a sparkle that I hadn't seen since he was 5 years old.

My relationship with both of my sons has miraculously changed in the past 6 months. We have a feeling of joy in our home like never before and there are no longer big arguments. We have eye contact with each other frequently and we really enjoy being together as a family. We are spending more time together, talking and playing games. And as I let them know our family needs, they are choosing to help out by doing their part, rather than me making a list for them and threatening to take their phone if they don't. It has been fun, and a little scary, to let go and watch them become the individuals that God created them to be, separate from me.

I am still new at this joy-filled parenting, but the results have been so rewarding that I will never go back to the old ways of controlling my teens. I just wish I had learned these skills when they were younger!

What a wonderful change from when Lisa first joined our Joy Group and humbly confessed, "I have messed up my kids and I need help." I will scatter more of Lisa's stories throughout the book as we see how she applied what she was learning. We will cover various topics and skills that Lisa used to help bring about changes. Lisa has been an inspiration to me and others as each week she tells us how life in her family is changing. During the week Lisa asks for help when she recognizes that her joy is slipping. She sends out group texts asking for prayer or answers to questions. Lisa has a community who is learning about joy with her. She has a safe place in which to open up and be real so that the relational skills become heart knowledge instead of just head knowledge. This safe and joy-filled community is an important part of Lisa's story. It's something all of us need.

Shawnda

Shawnda has lots of stories; she's been working on joy longer. As a former home school parent, Shawnda brings a slightly different perspective to the relational dynamics with a teen/young adult. All of us have learned from hearing how Shawnda has applied joy-filled teen parenting with her son, Trey. But like Lisa, Shawnda's parenting style was very different before learning about relational joy and the brain science. Shawnda and Trey butted heads quite a bit. Shawnda had a lot of rules and lectures were frequent. She fretted over dishes in the sink, homework, and un-mowed lawns. Her focus was also on how to solve problems and how to get Trey to do what the family required. Somewhere along the way, Shawnda had forgotten to look at Trey's heart. Applying the skills that we will look at here changed Shawnda and Trey's relationship.

Because Shawnda had worked so hard on acquiring the joy and brain skills, during our joy-filled community time, her stories gave substance to what Lisa needed to change and practice. Along the way, in addition to practicing new skills, both moms and their spouses sought healing for their own unresolved wounds. Taking old wounds to Jesus, discovering where He was in the event, and hearing Him say the truth about it diminishes the possibility of triggers that interrupt relationships.[2] Triggers come from unresolved wounds that cause us to feel that the person in front of us is the problem. The real problem is something from our past, but we usually do not realize the past is related. Here is one of Shawnda's stories about how things changed with Trey when Jesus healed one of her old past wounds:

Healing Prayer

For 19 years we were a homeschooling family. It was a very satisfying part of our early years of life, but I found it more and more difficult for myself as they all entered their teen years. I especially found it tough with my son at times. There was a season, before Joy-Filled Relationships, that was very hard and I did a lot of blowing up at Trey. As I learned about

---

[2] For more information on Immanuel prayer see *Share Immanuel* booklet, Wilder & Coursey, lifemodelworks.org

Immanuel prayer in Barbara's small group, I realized this explosive behavior was damaging our relationship. After a particularly hard day I went to Barbara for help. She led me through a prayer time, asking Jesus to show me what He wanted me to know about being so upset. Jesus showed me a memory. In this memory, I had been humiliated in front of others and the person upset with me turned around and walked away, leaving me upset and feeling alone, amid a crowd of people. Jesus showed me He was there with me, facing me and not walking away. He told me the lie that I was believing about myself was that I was unimportant. Jesus told me I was important to Him and bonded with me in this old memory.

I realized that during my fights with my son, he also would turn away to disengage from my yelling. This action triggered me and made it worse! Now I knew what was going on—I had been applying past emotions to present happenings and losing all relationship in the process. I went home and immediately told my son about my prayer time and what Jesus showed me. I asked for his forgiveness for my past behavior and he gladly gave it. Since then, we have had disagreements and at times I have been overwhelming to him. He would still practice disengaging, but I no longer needed to blow up about it because Jesus had healed the old wound. Now I can calm myself, practice pausing, and allow tension to subside while we work through any situation.

As we can see from her story, Shawnda noticed clues that she might be triggered because her emotions were way out of proportion to the circumstance with Trey. After Jesus healed the wound, less triggering meant less conflict. Less conflict makes relating a whole lot easier.

My Journey

Along with Lisa, Shawnda, and others, I have some stories of my own. Although my children are now grown with children of their own, God taught me some of what I will share here back when mine were teens. It was not an easy journey, but as He promised, whatever we learn will help us to help others. Little did I know that one of my most wonderful, painful stories would be with a precious teenage granddaughter. She has given me permission to share our story, a story of grace and redemption. Our story is about seeing a teen acting out but approaching her behavior as a symptom of avoiding pain instead of only looking at her actions. Instead of discipline, Rose needed to learn what to do with her emotional pain. For sure the behavior was not OK, but there was more going on under the surface. Rose's story will be told in a couple of places, including the joyful ending. We pray it will be helpful to hear and bring hope to any in similar circumstances.

The life-changing stories and information we will see here share some common factors. The learning and practicing took place in safe, authentic, joy-filled community, the foundation for learning to apply life-changing information. Associating with people who have the brain/relational skills we are missing proves to improve our families, our lives, and our relationships. People who are humble and teachable learn quickly. People who open up and ask for help, admitting their messes, find hope. How we share and transfer what we have learned is vital. And—allowing Jesus to heal our unresolved pain frees us to relate differently. Being willing to grow and change brings about joy-filled relationships with our teens.

CHAPTER TWO: HOW DOES RELATIONAL JOY WORK WITH THE BRAIN?

Joy, as far as the brain is concerned, means, "Someone is glad to be with me. I'm the sparkle in someone's eye." Joy does NOT mean everything is happy. Really getting this definition is vital for us to be able to experience relationships that are authentic, meaningful, and life-changing. We have to know (and communicate to others) that someone is glad to be with us regardless of circumstances or intense emotions. This concept goes against what most of us believe and practice. We are not accustomed to being glad to be together when things are not going well. Lisa's testimony of how she used to relate to her boys is a good example of not being glad to be together when situations are difficult. We saw the contrast of how Lisa now approaches her teens with joy.

I encourage all of us to let this definition of joy soak into our awareness. We will see changes when we keep it in the forefront of our minds and hearts. Real joy will change how we approach our teens because being glad to be together cannot be faked. If by chance our motive for being with our teen is because we want to fix or just correct them, it will not be sensed as real joy. If we are holding a grudge or harboring bitterness, we cannot pretend to be glad to be together. Genuine love shows up on our faces; so does pretending.

Joy Takes Two

By its very definition, joy takes two. There has to be another person for us to be glad with. The good news is that Jesus can be the other, and He is always glad to be with us no matter what. Hearing that Jesus is always glad to be with us might take some getting used to. Some of us have been taught that Jesus is quite upset with us when we are not OK or we have done wrong. I'm not saying it's OK to sin; I'm saying He's there and glad to be with us to help us get through upset or sin. I was taught growing up that I better behave because God was watching. That idea gives the implication that He is out to get us. When I believed God was out to get me, it did not encourage me to want to be close to Him. Now I understand how big His grace and love are. Knowing grace and love encourages me to feel close. I don't see Jesus as frowning at me with displeasure and disapproval. I realize He loves me unconditionally and wants to be with me through whatever is going on. I behave because I love Him and I know He loves me. Love and grace is what we want our teens to know and experience.

No Condemnation

Take time to ponder that Jesus is always glad to be with us. Take time to consider the definition of Joy and study grace if you don't know what it truly is. Begin to separate conviction from condemnation. Conviction is when someone speaks to correct my *behavior*. Condemnation is when someone communicates that *I am bad* because of my behavior. There is a big difference. Some of us may fear conviction *and* condemnation because, while growing up, discipline mostly communicated condemnation. There was no separation between identity and behavior. We can't feel the difference.

Our words and even our voice tone can communicate the difference between condemnation and conviction. Calling a person *a liar* when they tell a lie is condemnation. Speaking to *lying* is conviction. Jesus will convict, but He won't condemn. His love will not change because He has to speak to our behavior.

Voice tone surrounding "correct" words easily communicates disgust, disapproval, or rejection when a teen needs to feel loved and accepted first. Throughout the book we will encounter ways to understand and practice grace instead of condemnation in our own lives and towards our teens. How we speak to, look at, and talk about our teens can determine if they are feeling condemned and judged. We want to learn grace as a vital part of joy-filled parenting with teens. Lisa has a story about realizing that she was judging her teen over a TV show he was absorbed with.

Grimm Story

Focusing on controlling my teenagers has been preventing me from enjoying time with them. Jonathan, my 15 year old, started watching a recorded TV show this summer that was extremely violent. He enjoyed it so much he watched it several times a day. I felt my stress level rise each time I saw him watching it because I felt there were better ways for him to use his time. I refused to watch the show with him as a protest that it was not a good influence on him. When he wasn't watching it, I found that we had nothing to talk about and we were not connecting at all. We had nothing to say to each other. Finally, in an effort to value the relationship with him over the problem, I decided to join him in the show. I found that, though it was violent, it was actually a very well done show and I started enjoying it. It became something that was drawing us closer together. We could talk about it outside of the viewing and it created a sense of shared fun together.

As Lisa kept in mind that relationships are more important than problems, she was able to change her mind and look at the situation with grace instead of judgment and fear.

Building Joy

Building joy and being in joy with teens (and others) is non-verbal. Joy is best built eye-to-eye and face-to-face, but we don't only have to be looking at each other all the time. There are various ways to communicate that we are glad to be with someone. Voice tones, smiles, and proper touches communicate joy. Pleasant smells, food, and having fun together build joy. Pets, babies, and elderly people bring joy. Joy is all about giving life to those around us as we communicate that we are glad to be with them. When circumstances are not happy, we can still be glad to be together.

As we build joy, something happens in our brain. Later we will look more closely at how the brain works, but for now, we can realize that being glad to be together enables our brains to handle distress. The more joy we have, the easier it is to stay relational under stress. When emotions are intense, joy helps us calm. When we can be glad to be with our teen "no matter what" we help them learn joy, calming, and how to stay relational when circumstances are not going well. Growing joy is good news!

Lisa's story about following Jason out to the garage is a good example of being glad to be together in spite of her teen's emotions. When Lisa just smiled and said, "No words," Jason melted a bit and the rebuilding began. Over the next weeks Lisa continued to communicate more non-verbally. Her smiles were genuinely joyful because her heart was so motivated to reconnect with her teens. Slowly but surely, joy and synchronizing built a new bridge between Lisa and Jason. (We will look closer at synchronizing in the next chapter.)

Five Levels in the Brain

What we have been looking at about relational joy takes place in the right side of our brain. In order to better understand why we are even looking at the brain, let's take a look at this chart. The chart can be a referral page for understanding and further study. Just glance back at it as we go through this chapter and the next. Even though it's a bit technical, it's well worth the effort to get a basic understanding of the brain science. The first four levels on the chart are on the right side of our brain. Level 5 is on the left side which is not part of relating. The left side is about logic and words. Keep this distinction in mind as we go.

What Does It Take to Thrive?[3]

THRIVING	NOT THRIVING	BRAIN LEVEL
1) A Place to Belong—**I know I'm loved.**	Insecure Attachment-- **fear based relating**	The Attachment Center (Thalamus) **Who or what is important to me?**
2) Receiving & giving life—**I can live unselfishly.**	Self-centered—**It's all about me and my fear.**	The Evaluation Center (Amygdala) **What is Good, Bad, Scary?**
3) Synchronizing with others and God. **Return-to-joy from upset. And Forgiveness**	**Loss** of Synchronization with others and/or my brain itself de-synchronizes.	The Sharing Center (Right Cingulate) **Where we share Peace, Joy, or Distress with others and God.**
4) Maturity—**I can act like myself.**	Immaturity—**I'm missing some relational skills and I melt down easily.**	The Joy Center (Right Pre-frontal-cortex) **Where joy is built, my identity, and my attention to the World**
5) Knowing My Heart—**I can walk what I talk.**	Living by the Flesh— **I'm trying to figure things out by myself.**	The Logic Center (Left Hemisphere) **Words, logic, reasoning.** **My explanations of my life**

It's not necessary to memorize this chart. It's a simplified way to look at some basics about the relational brain and how God designed it to work in relationships. I want us to realize the importance of the Right Hemisphere and how practical it is. Knowing how it works will help us

---

[3] Chart from Dr. Wilder's THRIVE Conference. For more information on the brain science, see my book *Joy-Filled Relationships*.

relate better with our teens. For further study, most of the books mentioned in footnotes or on the resource page at the end will have more detail. For now let's look at some reasons that the Right Hemisphere is so important.

The Fast Track

The right side of our brain processes much faster than conscious thought and that is very important to realize. What we have trained into the right side, the Fast Track, will greatly determine our responses and reactions as we relate to God and others. Because the process is so fast, there is not time to choose. If we want responses to be loving, kind, and gentle those qualities must be what is trained into the Fast Track.[4] We cannot pass gentle responses on to our teens if we are not gentle protectors ourselves.

We are all born as "predators" and we must be trained to be gentle protectors.[5] Being born as "predators" means that our bent is to be selfish and to want our own way. Jesus came to show us how to live as He does with the Father. He wants us to be kind, loving, sharing, caring, patient, and slow to anger. Most of us know verses that admonish us to show this kind of character but perhaps we don't realize the brain is involved. God designed the brain to be trained so that we *become* the kind of person that responds lovingly instead of having to grit our teeth and strive to keep control so we won't respond as a "predator."[6] Dallas Willard puts it this way, "To succeed in keeping the law one must aim at something other and something more. One must aim to become *the kind of person* from whom the deeds of the law naturally flow."[7]

Learn the Skills

If we did not learn gentle protector skills during childhood, we will need a joyful community to help us learn them now. A joyful community

---

[4] See *RARE Leadership* for more detail. www.lifemodel.org
[5] See *Joy Starts Here* for more detail. www.lifemodel.org
[6] *Joy Starts Here*, Wilder, Coursey, Khouri, Sutton, Shepherd's House, 2013 www.joystartshere.com
[7] *The Divine Conspiracy*, Dallas Willard, Harper San Francisco, 1998, page 142

is one like the one Lisa, John, and Shawnda are in. The group is a safe place to show weakness because there will be no condemnation for not being OK. In a joyful community people are glad to be together, they are teachable, and they are humble. They aren't afraid to let their weaknesses and hurts be known. They want to grow and they are patient with others wherever others are in their journey. A joy-filled community also speaks the truth in love when necessary. People help each other learn to receive correction without being defensive. And of course such a community prays for one another and helps out when help is needed. In order to function well in these areas, the group must have some leaders with maturity. It also helps growth if there are multi-generations in the community.

The skills to become gentle responders cannot be learned from a book or videos. We need to be with people who have the skills. In order to help our teens and live in joy-filled parenting, God will have to work on us first. Allowing the Holy Spirit to work on us is a worthy goal.

God is very willing to help us with this worthy goal. He knows all about the family in which we grew up. He understands what skills and maturity we are missing. He knows that when we were young, we grew our identity from what we saw on others' faces. God designed babies and children to learn who they are through joy, not fear or anger. If we grew up in a low-joy environment, we likely felt unwanted, alone, and unloved. Low joy makes it more difficult to handle distress. What we missed affects our relationships and our parenting. God wants to heal our hurts, help us get unstuck, and help us grow so that we can have a joy-filled family.

Who is My Teen?

Not only do babies learn who they are from the faces around them, teens also get their "older" identity from what they see on the faces around them. Shawnda has a great story that illustrates a simple way that we can help our teens read something positive on our faces.

Good Thoughts

Trey bought a big monster truck. He was so excited about it and took every opportunity to talk to me about its engine and body type. I listened to talk of carburetors, how many liters, connectors and pistons, brakes, and tires. I knew nothing about these things. At any rate, I knew he wanted to share and that I needed to stay connected and relational. As he would describe the latest item he wanted to add, or that needed to be fixed, I decided to delight in his excitement. I thought about how proud I was of him having bought it himself, and I thought about all that he was learning on his own about such a vehicle. While he was talking to me I would synchronize my face with his, whether it was happy or intense or frustrated. This helped me to stay in the present and be engaged without leaving him feeling as if I wasn't interested. I also pictured Trey as he was around the age of four, cute and adorable. I believe these good thoughts showed up on my face. Two years and about a million dollars later, he decided he should sell it. I was thankful to say the least!

After hearing this story several moms have found it easy to think these kinds of good thoughts while listening to their teens. What a great, non-verbal way to communicate how much we love someone.

The Joy Center in the Brain

Let's look more closely at the place in our brains where we build joy, the right prefrontal cortex. It is right behind the right eye. We call it the Joy Center. (Level 4 on the chart) When a baby is born this Joy Center is there but not developed. Both the size and capacity of the Joy Center are determined by joy in the first year or so of life. It becomes 35% of the adult brain. The good news is that the Joy Center can grow throughout life, so regardless of how much joy we or our teen got in the early years, we can work on growing joy now.

Earlier we looked at how to build joy and that doing so is non-verbal. Because the Joy Center is so important and a big percentage of the brain, we want to grow a lot of joy so the Joy Center can handle distress.[8] The

---

[8] See my book *Joy-Filled Relationships* for more information on the first years.

size and capacity of the Joy Center determine how well we handle distress. Here are a couple of analogies that can help us visualize how joy and distress are related. Shawnda's analogy pictures the Joy Center like a bank.

The joy contained in our Joy Bucket is like money in a bank. How much we can withdraw depends on how much we have and the intensity of the moment. And just as having some money in the bank brings security, joy in relationships also brings security.

The other analogy pictures the Joy Center as a bucket:

As the buckets illustrate, a full Joy Bucket makes it easier to handle distresses that are common to life. And when the Joy Bucket is not big and full, we become overwhelmed by distress. The result of overwhelm is that parts of our brain "melt down" or go "off." The brain de-synchronizes. The first part to go is the Left side (Level 5 on the chart) where we have logic, reasoning, and words. Lectures and instructions are useless when the Left side is off. Words are meaningless and teens will only get more frustrated if we talk too much while their Logic Center is melted down.

De-synchronization of the Brain

When the brain de-synchronizes further, the teen loses many functions other than words and reasoning. The Joy Center (the Joy Bucket) on the right side is next to go, which causes them to lose impulse control, social behavior, goal-directed behavior, focus, maturity, and the ability to stay relational under distress. They are no longer able to act like themselves. They need someone who can be glad to be with them *in* the distress to help them calm and get re-synchronized. Being able to be with someone who is distressed requires the "bigger brain" to have the capacity and skills to handle what is going on. This is why it is so important for us parents to work on our own skills and healing. Unhealed wounds cause triggers; lacking skills limits capacity. Both escalate conflict. Our teens will benefit from us being able to handle difficult situations.

If we as parents or the teens have "melted down," no problems will get solved until the brain is "back on," re-synchronized. The brain circuits that regulate relating are temporarily off. These Relational Circuits work the same for all ages.

Relational Circuits

Have you ever tried to talk to your teen when they were tired, hungry, or grumpy? What about when they seem annoyed at you? Maybe you noticed they wouldn't make eye contact. What about when you ask them to do something with you and they don't want to? These are some of the signs that the Relational Circuits (RCs) are off in the brain.

Let's look at a contrast of RCs off and RCs on:

When Our Relational Circuits Are Off	When Our Relational Circuits Are On
We feel irritable and grouchy	We can suffer well even if upset
We feel annoyed	We can be more patient
Our mind is locked onto something upsetting	Our mind is more peaceful
We don't want to be with someone we usually like	We want to be with people and interact
We want a person, problem, or feeling to go away	We are willing to work through a problem
We don't want to listen to anyone else.	We care about what is going on with others
We might be more aggressive than usual	We are able to listen and wait to speak

As you look at this list, which side would you prefer to be on when you are talking with your teen? Learning to recognize that RCs are off, and getting them back on, is life-changing. Many problems arise from trying to work through something when the RCs are off. Read this list again. Get a sense of how to recognize when yours are off and when others' are off. When the RC's are off, we have also lost all the functions in the Joy Center that we looked at on the previous page. Go back and read that list again.

Looking at these lists we can see that it's possible for a teenager to mostly *live* with the RCs off, especially at home. If families want to improve relationships, it's vital for everyone to know about, begin to notice, and live with the Relational Circuits on. When the RCs are off it is useless to try to solve a problem, discipline anyone, or have a discussion.

We can't settle our disagreements and our misunderstandings when we are not glad to be together and able to act like ourselves. When the

Relational Circuits are off, we are reduced to living out of the back of the brain with *fear* as the focus and motivator. Fear can trigger anger. Problems will be larger than relationships. We cannot hear lectures or see the other person's perspective. We are likely to say something that makes the situation worse. Lots of grace is needed later because we should not believe hurtful things others say when their RCs are off.

Cool off and get the RCs on before engaging in a discussion. Getting them back on is easy when we are willing, and it will make a difference even if it's just the parent who has theirs on. When the time is right, we can teach the teens about RCs and how much better life works when having them on.

Here is another story from Shawnda that happened before Trey bought his monster truck. This story helps us see how Shawnda was able to talk to Trey about one of her old memories involving big trucks. It was helpful to their relationship as they went back and forth and Shawnda purposed to notice the state of her RCs.

Relational Circuits

When Trey was 17 he decided to buy a truck. We sat together and he told me all the details of what type of truck he wanted. It would be big; lifted tall; have a big engine that would rumble; etc. As he was describing this truck I was reminded of a time in my past that included a truck of this nature. For me it was a very ugly, traumatic time that I didn't want to be reminded of. I told him that I thought it was possible such a truck might trigger me and I may not respond in a friendly manner at times. He understood after I shared a few more details and politely asked me this question: "Will you try to think of me and not old memories?" I said yes, I would try to recognize when I felt my relational circuits were dimming and let him know.

Jesus is relational

Another reason for learning to keep our RCs on is that Jesus is a relational being and we will not be able to hear Him easily if the RCs are off. Think about how Jesus interacted with His disciples. He was glad to be with them even when they messed up. He took Peter back to his denial and healed the rift that Peter was feeling. On the Cross Jesus thought about Mary and asked John to take care of her. He cared about the thief at His side. Read John Seventeen and notice His relationship with the Father and how He was thinking of us in the future.

Jesus wants an intimate, personal relationship with all of us. Making sure the RCs are on before praying or talking to Him changes the dynamics of our walk with God. We need our Joy Bucket full and our Relational Circuits on for any and all relational encounters. We are made to be in relationship.

Getting the Relational Circuits Back On

In this section I will be speaking mostly to parents as it might not be possible to "teach" all of this to our teens (or spouse) at first. We might have to wait until an opportune moment to share this new brain science. So each reader will have to discern how and when to share with others, especially family. The best way is to get our own skills going so that others notice a difference in our responses. As we learn to operate with RCs on, others will notice we are more gentle, more calm, and more glad to be with them regardless of circumstances and emotions.

Stimulate the Vagus Nerve

Dr. Wilder, Chris Coursey, and Ed Khouri of Life Model Works have developed some physical exercises that can re-synchronize the melted-down brain and get the RCs back on. The easiest is stimulating the vagus nerve. For this exercise, we tap with finger tips, about the speed of our heartbeat, on each side of the sternum while taking a deep breath. As we do this it stimulates the vagus nerve that runs from behind the ears down through the abdomen, touching all the organs inside. As we exhale the deep breath, we rub the chest and say this verse, "Whenever I'm afraid I will trust in You, O Lord." (Psalm 56:3) It's helpful to do this more than once and it can be done with one hand while driving.[9]

---

[9] Vagus nerve and appreciation exercises taken from *Joy Starts Here* by Dr. E. John Wilder, et al. www.lifemodelworks.org

Appreciation

Thinking about things that we appreciate (such as the beach, the mountains, flowers, babies, good relationships, or good memories) is another easy way to re-synchronize our brain. These things make us feel content, cozy, and make us smile. We almost make the sound, "ahhhh," as we breathe deeply and relax. It's good to give the appreciation picture a one-word name. Then we can have three or four appreciation moments that people around us know about so they can help us go there when we need to calm. If teens are willing, we can share our appreciation moments with each other and allow teens to help *us* calm—and vice versa.

If we really want to speed some joy building and brain changing we can do appreciation three times a day. If we had a difficult childhood that was not very joyful, over time appreciation will reset what has been our normal state which might have been fear-based rather than joy-based. Express appreciation three times a day with someone you are close to using this guideline: 3 x 3 x 3[10]

1. What I appreciate about my day.

2. What I appreciate about God.

3. What I appreciate about the person with whom I am sharing.

If three times three times three seems too much right now we can begin by expressing the three appreciations at least one time per day.

Finding Jesus

Taking a break and disengaging from stress for a short time is another way to help us calm and get our Relational Circuits on. We can then stimulate the vagus nerve or go to an appreciation memory. We can also ask Jesus, "Where are You in the room (car, etc.) with me right now?" (Matthew 1:23; Matthew 28:20; Hebrews 13:5)

---

[10] From *Joy Starts Here*

As we sense Jesus' presence we can ask Him, "What do You want me to know about this situation?" Most times He will meet us and help us relate better if we listen. Many of David's Psalms let us see how David laments and then hears God. Psalm 3:4 tells us that David cried out and God answered. Psalm 62:11 says, "Once God has spoken: Twice I have heard this: That power belongs to God. . ." Isaiah listens to the Lord in Chapter 6: verses 8 and 28:22. Paul's conversion is a good example of interacting with Jesus. (Acts 9: 4-5)   We see in Revelation 4:1 that John listened to the voice of Jesus.

Jesus is always glad to be with us. Think about the woman taken in adultery, (John 8:7) and the woman at the well, neither exactly in their finest moment. (John 4:26) As Creator, Jesus knows all about the brain science; He knows us and our situations, and He wants to help. He wants us to trust Him to be there and guide us when we ask and listen. (For more information and instruction on listening prayer see *Joyful Journey,* a great book on listening prayer and Immanuel Journaling.[11])

Too Much Intensity

Sometimes our emotions can be so intense that we find it difficult to self-calm. In these times we need help from someone who knows these skills. Being in a joy-filled community is a great place to find someone to help when we are overwhelmed. In two of my groups the ladies have all joined an app on their phones that enables us to group text and ask and give prayer, encouragement, and words of joy.

As we walk out daily relating with these new skills, it will become easier and easier to at least recognize that the Relational Circuits are dimming and about to go off. We will notice we've lost our peace; we will notice we are irritated. When we need outside help, it's time to text or call someone who has what we call "a bigger brain." A bigger brain is a person who can handle our emotions and help us return to acting like ourselves because they don't try to fix us or melt down themselves when they see

---

[11] *Joyful Journey, Listening to Immanuel,* Dr. Wilder, Anna Kang, John Loppnow, Sungshim Loppnow, Shepherd's House, 2015, www.lifemodelworks.org

upset. Bigger brains are not afraid of our need and they will help us calm. Meanwhile, until we are calm and relational, we will disengage from the conflict so as not to say unkind words and make things worse. We want to practice noticing and keeping our RCS on so that we can become the bigger brain to our teens. And it can be very interesting and positive if we allow our teen to be the "bigger brain" with *us* if we are upset.

Relationships are More Important than Problems

Because we really do not want to make things worse, remembering that relationships are more important than the problem will help motivate us to practice our budding relational skills. It makes a great card to put on the refrigerator: ***RELATIONSHIPS ARE MORE IMPORTANT THAN THE PROBLEM***. When we know and practice this truth, it can help us be "quick to hear, slow to speak, and slow to anger." (John 1: 19).

When God brings to mind that relationships are more important than the problem, if possible, we can pause and ask ourselves any of these kinds of questions: "Where is my focus? Is it on the relationship or the problem?" "What is my teen's heart like?" "What do I need to do to be able to respond kindly and see my teen's perspective?" "Is this a battle I need to let go of?" "Is what I'm about to say going to cause more conflict and make things worse?"

Remembering these kinds of questions makes it easier to pause before harming. There may very well be something that needs addressing, but we don't try to solve or address problems until everyone is calm with RCs on.

Pausing and asking ourselves these questions reminds us that we care about the relationship. When our RCs are off and we are reacting unkindly, our focus is on the problem, not the person's heart. Parents will see improvement with their teens when they learn these relational skills and re-train their Fast Tracks to be gentle responders.

CHAPTER THREE: SYNCHRONIZING, ANOTHER PART OF THE RELATIONAL CIRCUITS

Synchronizing is an important brain skill that helps us see others' perspectives. Seeing your teen's perspective will smooth many bumps along the way. Synchronizing takes place when we share the same energy level with someone; when we are on the same wave length. What we are sharing is joy (glad to be together), peace (quiet), or distress (negative emotions).

We can share different levels of joy—high joy is when we share fun things, excitement, laughter, or lots of smiles. A quiet level of being glad to be together might be sitting together on the deck, watching a camp fire, or quietly scratching our teen's back.

Peace is when we share that all is as it should be, no conflict; all is well. The Bible calls this "Shalom." It's like us to want to be at peace. When we sense that we or our teen have lost our peace, it should be a signal to us—like when a referee blows his whistle in a game—it's time to stop. It's time to discover what's going on; it's time to check the RCs. Paul tells us in Colossians 3: 15—"Let the peace of Christ rule in your heart."

Sharing distress with our teens can be more difficult than sharing joy and peace. Many of us avoid sharing distress of any kind with anyone. We will look further at sharing negative emotions shortly. In Chapter Five we will look at some relational brain skills that make it easier to synchronize distress.

When our teen is low energy, quiet, subdued, or occupied, we want to approach them with that same level of energy. Interrupting, blasting, or jumping on someone is not synchronizing. Badgering a teen to get our point across is not synchronizing. Let's look at one of Shawnda's stories about how she first began to practice synchronizing with Trey after she learned its importance.

Synchronizing

As I was growing up I learned a very special skill. It's called yelling. Whenever you wanted someone's attention or needed their presence, you yelled for them. So, what did I do as a parent of 3? I yelled of course! I made the demand for their presence and never took the time to find out what they were doing when I needed them. This was an "it's all about me" attitude.

As I learned in Joy-Filled Relationships about synchronizing I realized this skill was not relational. One day, at the bottom of our stairs, I was about to yell for my son to come to me. I paused and had this amazing thought, "Yelling is not relational. Go to him."

Up the stairs I went and to his bedroom. Trey always keeps his door open and his bed faces the doorway. I stood silently until he paused his video game and asked me what I needed. I asked if he had time to talk; he said, "Sure." I proceeded to ask what I needed to ask and he answered politely and away I went. I felt very satisfied and he felt very respected.

Since that day I have always gone to him and we as a family have a new expectation, go to the person to whom you wish to speak...no more yelling.

Just as Shawnda took note of Trey's energy level and how he was occupied, it's helpful to notice the energy level when our teens return home. Are they up for a hug and chatter? Do they need time to unwind? Are they down because they're having a bad day? Is the energy level higher because they are excited to share something from their day?

When we have this skill in our Fast Track to notice our teen's face and body language, the teen will feel loved, accepted, and understood. They are less likely to feel that we are pushing ourselves or an agenda onto them.

Synchronizing is very unselfish and done best face-to-face, communicating with eyes that light up, welcoming body language, and kind voice tone. Dr. Wilder says that synchronizing is like good music—

right timing, right intensity, and right tone. Picture synchronized swimming in the Olympics. Picture dancing, or playing in an orchestra.

Failure to Synchronize

Failure to synchronize is the opposite of harmony in an orchestra. It feels like the discord of an un-tuned guitar—bad timing, bad intensity, and bad tone. It's easy to forget to synchronize and it's easy to get preoccupied and just not notice where our teen is at the moment. Not synchronizing is painful, so we want to practice and get good at this skill. When we forget to synchronize, teens can feel misunderstood. If it accumulates over time they could even feel unloved, alone, afraid, or unwanted. These feelings undermine relationships and we need help and healing for these kinds of hurts.

Sharing a Mind

The ability to synchronize is a brain function that takes place in the Sharing Center (Level 3 on the chart in Chapter Two). In addition to sharing energy, timing, intensity, and tone, when we synchronize with our teens, we share a mind with them. That's how we see their perspective; it's literally a physical thing. Our brains are connected. Our focus is unselfishly on them and what's going on in their mind and heart.

The Sharing Center also allows us to share a mind and synchronize with God. Just think about that for a minute. We can know what God thinks about a situation. We can realize He is on our wave length. We can see His perspective. When we feel at odds with our teens' attitudes, words or actions, sharing a mind with God will bring peace and rest when we see how God sees. When we are upset ourselves, sharing a mind with God will allow us to ask Him about what's troubling us and see His perspective. Finding out what He wants us to know about a situation helps us grow and heal and relate differently so that we become better parents. Look at II Kings 6: 15-17 for a good example of sharing a mind with God.

Synchronizing Negative Emotions

We can also share a mind with our teen when we notice our teen is upset and experiencing a negative emotion. During negative emotions, one person has to be the "bigger brain" with better skills in order to help calm the negative feelings and get back to joy (being glad to be together). If neither has a well-trained brain, the negative emotions get amplified and conflict will escalate. The Relational Circuits will go off. Now the relating is similar to two kindergarteners in a sandbox. We have a parent and a teen who have both lost their maturity in the Joy Center. Neither is able to act like who they are. It's time to disengage and find someone to help. When the two are back to sharing joy, the joy will amplify and the energy will be pleasant and fun.

When the timing is right, and we are able to synchronize with our teen, be glad to be with them in the distress, and listen without fixing, they will feel validated and comforted. They understand that it's OK to not be OK. They feel known and seen. It's easier for them to acknowledge their needs and be willing to receive help.

It's easy to see how our relationships with our teens will transform if we practice synchronizing with them. We see from their perspective and take into account what is going on in their world. If the *behavior* is negative, we correct that at the right time, but if *feelings* are negative, we synchronize and stay glad to be together. (We will look at correction in a later chapter.)

Overwhelm

Synchronizing in the Sharing Center also helps us with another skill. When we have learned this skill, we can recognize if *we are overwhelming others*. Overwhelming others causes many relationship problems. Too much talking, too much drama, and too many intense emotions are common pathways to overwhelm. If a parent is overwhelming, teens will shy away from them. If a teen is overwhelming others, they might have fewer friends. They will need help and practice to learn to synchronize better.

In the *Appendix* there are some exercises that can help us learn to recognize when we are about to be overwhelmed or when we are overwhelming another. Noticing overwhelm in our teen or others is mostly done by learning to read subtle facial cues around the eyes. Body language can cue us in to what is going on with our teen. Awareness of the need and the practice of noticing overwhelm will greatly improve our relationships with our teens.

Practicing

So how can we learn to synchronize? It's best learned from someone who knows how. This is the importance of our joyful communities. Like building joy, synchronizing takes place in the Fast Track (the brain's Right side), non-verbally, and faster than conscious thought. The interaction is done left-eye to left-eye faster than we can think. The reason the interaction is left-eye to left-eye is because the left side of our brain controls the right side of the body. So the synchronizing is going on right-brain to right-brain. Any time we can share energy levels and/or make eye contact with our teens, interaction between our two brains will take place. During any eye-to-eye sharing it's important to glance away and rest for a few seconds. Resting helps avoid overwhelm.

When we are synchronizing and sharing a mind, it's common to be unsure who started the interaction because the sharing is so fast. We often say, "He made me (smile, mad, sad.)" Here is a fun exercise to help **practice synchronizing and building joy**. Lisa and John do this exercise often with their teens. Doing this has helped Jason sleep better. We will notice in Lisa's stories that she asks Jason if he wants to synchronize in order to feel better after they've had conflict. The exercise can feel a bit strange at first, but trust that this will help everyone. If you are doing this exercise with a person to whom you are close, it can be done with two people.

The exercise forms bonds between those doing it.

1. Sit together as two or three and sit "knee-to-knee," face-to-face.

2. There will be no talking (but there might be giggling.)

3. You will look at each other left-eye to left-eye.

4. Notice how much the other is smiling and synchronize with their level of energy, size of the smile.

5. Glance away to rest and have seconds of quiet. Resume eye contact. Take about a total of two minutes for the exercise.

Sometimes we, or our teens, did not learn how to synchronize, build joy, and rest. Ideally these skills should be learned the first two years of life. It's not too late to learn the skills if we are willing to practice. When synchronizing is practiced with joy building and rest, we will see new, secure, joy-filled bonds built with our teens.

CHAPTER FOUR: EMOTIONAL MATURITY

Emotional maturity is a concept that more people need to know about and practice. Unlike spiritual maturity, emotional maturity has nothing to do with how much Scripture we know. It has nothing to do with chronological age. Emotional maturity means, *I am able to act like myself and stay relational regardless of intense emotions. I am able to keep my heart open even when emotions or circumstances are difficult.*

When emotionally mature, we have completed what we needed to *receive* from others and what we needed to *learn* during certain stages of life. In Chapter Seven there are detailed lists for three of the five stages that can help us evaluate maturity. The lists are divided into *Needs* for each stage and *Tasks* for each stage. Needs are "acquired" from those around us and Tasks are "required" that we learn. Using these lists we can discover what maturity skills are missing in our own lives as well as those that are missing in our teens' maturity. Don't get discouraged by what is missing. Growth is possible. For now we will look at an *overview* of emotional maturity.

Through understanding human development and places in Scripture, Dr. Wilder and others at Life Model Works came up with the five stages of emotional maturity that cover our lifetime. Infant stage goes from pre-birth to age four. Child stage is from age four to age thirteen. The adult stage begins around the age of thirteen and continues to the birth of the first child. The parent stage begins with the birth of the first child until the youngest child is into the adult stage. Elders are ready to help their communities after progressing through the needs and tasks required in all previous stages, and their youngest child is thirteen.

Maturity happens best when children/teens are reared with joy bonds in a joy-filled family. This means that regardless of age, interactions are based on everyone being glad to be together. Fear and anger are not the normal environment, and when conflict does arise, people want to work through the issues. Children/teens are more likely to grow well in a joy-filled environment.

Maturity Is Not About Value

Each stage of maturity builds on the previous stage and none can be skipped. When we look through the list of stages in Chapter Seven, we can know which stage we or our teen are in by the needs and tasks that have been mastered. Since chronological age may not correspond, realize there may be some "holes" within a previous stage because we or our teens didn't get some of the needs or learn some of the tasks. Recognizing the holes will help us know what we or our teen need to work on.

It's important to remember that what we have mastered or not mastered has nothing to do with value. We are valuable no matter the level of emotional maturity to which we have grown. Immaturity is not a club with which to hit someone over the head. We need patience, kindness, and help to mature and grow what's missing.

Two Kinds of Traumas

Ideally we should progress through the stages naturally as we grow up, but that is not always the case. Often what we are lacking is not from our own doing. We have holes in our maturity because those around us did not know certain skills and how to pass them on. We saw no model of the skill. Maybe we didn't get enough love, acceptance, or guidance. Some may not have had enough food and protection. We call these holes Type **A** traumas. Type **A** traumas are the **A**bsence of good things that we needed growing up. These kinds of traumas can be difficult to recognize because we may not even be aware that we had an unmet need. Or we might know there were unmet needs, but we didn't know they could affect us so deeply. We have buried the pain and see our past as unimportant, best forgotten, or maybe even normal.

We have some holes because we were disciplined badly or abused. We call these Type **B** traumas. Type **B** traumas are **B**ad things that happened to us. Type **B** are the kinds of traumas that we think of when we hear the word trauma. We know it's bad. What we don't realize sometimes is that the definition of a trauma is much broader than abuse. A trauma is any event that *"leaves us feeling upset and alone."* Many things happen growing up that leave us feeling upset and alone, even such things as not being chosen for a team at school. Whichever kind of traumas that we've experienced leaves holes in our maturity. These holes are missing needs and skills that bring pain and cause relationship problems. We are stuck at a younger age in emotional immaturity.

Different Solutions

The solution for each of these traumas is a little different. Chapter Seven will help us see what we and our teens are missing. When we know what is missing and why, we can get unstuck. Jesus can heal the bad things that happened, and in joyful communities we can find people who know the skills we need to learn.

In both cases where we did not get what we needed in childhood and/or bad things happened, we will need authentic, joy-filled community to help us fill in the blanks. We need support within a safe community because filling in the blanks is painful. We need to feel safe to share our pain and know we will be comforted and heard without condemnation. As we hear others share how they grew and received healing, we have hope.

Parents who are humble and teachable can get healed and learn the missing skills and pass them on to their teens. Most of the skills are learned non-verbally and that's a plus. It does help to have some information and words for the skills, but as parents learn they will *model* the new skills. Eventually when teens sense a difference in the parents, it will be easier to "teach" the information about the skills.

Parents cannot take their children to a maturity level past their own level of growth, so that makes it vital that parents are willing to have others with information and missing skills to encourage and help them grow. Sometimes we fail to realize that teens want to be successful adults. I've found that knowing what maturity entails gives teens a kind of road map. Lisa has a great story about how she introduced a missing adult skill to her two teens.

Mutual Satisfaction

My oldest son developed quite a self-centered attitude from being the favorite over the years. The family had become centered around him and I didn't know what to do to change the course. Specifically, he was playing music loudly on his phone as he traveled throughout the house and was quite offended when we would ask him to turn it down or to put in his ear buds. Barbara suggested I call a family meeting and begin introducing our teenagers to the levels of emotional maturity, specifically the stage of Adulthood. (They loved the idea of being an adult and were interested in how to achieve that status.) In our meeting we brought up the adult skill of creating Mutual Satisfaction.

I invited sharing re how each family member felt we were doing as a family at creating mutual satisfaction in the area of sound/noise in common areas of the home. The boys shared their thoughts and my husband and I shared, too. Then I asked everyone to share ideas of how we could create mutual satisfaction in our family in the common areas. We voted on the ideas and came up with a list of behaviors we adopted as a family. Since the meeting, our oldest son has made huge improvements in sacrificing his own desires. This is the first time he has been personally motivated, willing, and on board in actually making personal changes and sacrifices for our family. He seemed motivated by the idea that he is doing it to become an adult.

We have continued the family meetings concerning mutual satisfaction and are currently addressing how to create mutual satisfaction in terms of "upkeep of our home/common areas." They boys are helping out with cleaning and house projects for the first time without complaining and grumbling!

That's a great story about modeling and coming to mutual satisfaction over an issue. Guidelines for Lisa and John' family meeting included having one person talk at a time and giving all a chance to speak. John used this time to explain about Relational Circuits and share with the teens how to do the vagus nerve exercise so that everyone could be sure their RCs stayed on. After their discussion Lisa wrote out their decisions about how to practice what they'd agreed on. She posted it in the kitchen. The teens had a voice in discussing, planning, and implementing mutual satisfaction.

Getting Unstuck

It's good to hear how Lisa's and Shawnda's families have seen changes with their teens. Both have sought help for missing skills and then applied them. In addition to learning missing skills, healing from their own unresolved wounds is also part of what parents have to face. That's good news for those who are willing to do what it takes to get unstuck. We saw in one of Shawnda's stories how she took a Type **B** trauma to Jesus and He healed the wound. Jesus showed Shawnda through listening prayer that she was not alone at the time of the trauma. He, Immanuel, our omnipresent Lord was there with her. Since He is not bound by time, Jesus can take us back to unresolved hurts and show us where He was. As He has for both Shawnda and Lisa, He can show us what that event caused us to believe about ourselves and then tell us His truth about the lies we believed. This process is how we get unstuck from Type **B** traumas. We are set free to begin growing again. There is pain involved when looking at a wound, but the pain is worth the effort when we see our lives and those of our teens begin to change.[12]

Growth and Maturity Not Automatic

Healing traumas does not automatically guarantee growth in maturity or character. Maturity and character take time and a loving, safe, and joy-filled community. Maturity and character grow slowly because we have to acquire needs and skills that we missed out on growing up—our Type **A** traumas. As we have looked at, to replace the **A**bsence of good things we need people who love and accept us and are able to build bonds that help us feel connected. We need patient people with enough maturity to put up with us learning and growing. It can be messy. As we grow, we can't look at ourselves, our spouses, or our teens and see only what is lacking. We need people with grace for our stumbling as we learn the missing skills. We started by getting unstuck through Immanuel healing, and we will continue to find healing there.

---

[12] *Share Immanuel* booklet and Dr. Lehman's books, excellent resources about Immanuel prayer, are on the Resource page. The Appendix has a few details as well.

To grow character and maturity we also need a joy-filled community based on gentleness towards weakness.[13] Missing what we should have received and/or being left upset and alone is very painful. Pain often makes us feel weak so we try to hide it. Not being at a stage that corresponds with our chronological age makes us appear weak. Most of us believe that pain and weakness are to be avoided at all costs. In order to grow, everyone must feel safe to open up and learn to acknowledge the needs, hurts, and weaknesses. In order to get unstuck, we have to stop avoiding pain and learn to suffer well.

---

[13] *Joy Starts Here* , Wilder, Coursey, Khouri, and Sutton, is all about gentleness towards weakness.

CHAPTER FIVE: AVOID PAIN OR SUFFER WELL.

Suffering well means that *we can stay relational and act like ourselves during pain and difficulties*. We've been taught that pain is bad and must be avoided, but most pain only lasts about ninety seconds. Try this quick exercise:

Set the stopwatch on your phone. Close your eyes. Think about a time when you felt embarrassed or humiliated. Start the stopwatch. Let yourself feel the feeling as long as it lasts. When you are not feeling it anymore, check the watch. Don't go by thoughts about the event, but the actual feelings. Most emotions last about 90 seconds.

Most teens are good at avoiding pain. Most have learned that art from the adults around them. Everyone will need support while learning to stop avoiding emotional pain. Habitually avoiding pain causes addictions, and wanting to prevent addictions should help motivate us. When we avoid pain, we turn to things that temporarily ease the pain. After a while these pleasures or dulling agents become what we are bonded to instead of people. Since God made us to be relational, when relationships don't work, we will try to find something to take the place of that lack of joy. Instead of helping, addictions add to relationship problems. What we are craving is someone who is glad to be with us—joy! Those things we turn to instead are not satisfying; they are false joy.[14]

Find Out Why

When teens are involved in addictions, accusations and condemnation fly all around everywhere. Parents focus on what the teen is *doing* instead of "why" they are doing it. It is likely that the root of the problem is avoiding emotional pain even though there may be no conscious memory of an unresolved wound. Teens often fear to look at, talk about, or feel what happened even if it is remembered. Toxic shame and/or guilt are

---

[14] See *Joy Starts Here* and equippinghearts.com for more information on addictions.

likely in the mix. If a teen grew up without validation and comfort when they hurt, it's very likely that they will turn to addictions to cover the pain.

Attackers and Pouters

Some people who avoid pain withdraw and pout, while others avoid pain by bullying others. Bullying (attacking, accusing, yelling, blaming, turning back on the other) keeps others away so we don't have to look at what might be wrong in our lives. Whether a teen withdraws or attacks, the purpose is to avoid pain. Regardless of the reason for the pain—unmet needs or painful traumas—when we avoid pain we stop maturing where the pain originated. Emotional maturity does not match the chronological age.

So what do we need? First, it will help to learn the truth about pain so we can suffer well. This is a difficult subject that not too many want to look at. My book, *Re-Framing Your Hurts: Why You Don't Have to Avoid Emotional Pain* is a broad study on the truth about emotional pain and what to do about it. It will help if parents learn to suffer well so teens will see a model for not avoiding pain. If addictions are already in full force, everyone will need help from a good counselor who knows Immanuel Prayer.

Don't Fix Pain

As we learn to look at pain differently, we all need someone who is glad to be with us *in* the pain without trying to fix it. Fixing others' hurts is a difficult habit to break. Most of us use various methods to try to fix someone's pain so we feel less uncomfortable. For Christians the most common fix is to tell someone the truth. Or we might quote Scripture. Or give them a book to read. Many make a joke to stop pain. Even passing tissue to someone who starts to cry can make them stop feeling what they need to feel.

With teens it's easy to lecture, shame, or even blame them for their feelings. It's easy to tune teens out and ignore them by focusing on trying to fix behavior. None of these really fix; they generally make things worse. Teens want to be heard and understood, even if we don't agree with them.

Here is an exercise that might help break the habit of trying to fix:

> Stop for a moment and consider ways you try to fix your teen when you see him or her hurting. Write them down.
>
> _____
>
> _____
>
> How do you feel when someone tries to fix you instead of just sitting with you and listening to you?
>
> _____
>
> _____
>
> What do you want someone to do for you when you are hurting?
>
> _____
>
> _____
>
> Do you need to sit down with your teen or someone else and share how you can help each other better when hurting?
>
> _____
>
> _____

Let's be open to realizing when we are trying to fix our teen (or anyone). The reason we fix is to make *ourselves* more comfortable. Let's learn to sit with someone in their pain, validate and comfort them, before we give solutions.

Validation and Comfort

Validation and comfort sum up what helps the most when a teen is hurting. Validation communicates to a hurting or even disgruntled teen that we can see that they are hurting or frustrated. "This is really big. I can see how it's hurting you. I'm so sorry." "I can see how frustrated you are right now. How can I help?" Teens feel understood and heard. Validation is part of synchronizing that we looked at in Chapter Three. It's not psychobabble; it's a skill that brings connection.

Sometimes it's better not to use words at first, but validating words are more about the tone of voice. We validate what our teen is feeling, but not necessarily that the feelings are true. The feelings might not be true, but the hurting or frustrated teen does not want to hear that during the pain. They want to feel heard and understood. The last thing teens want is a lecture.

Comfort comes after validation and is more non-verbal. It's about voice tone, safe touches, body language, facial expressions, and listening. It's important to remember we communicate non-verbally through the Fast Track side of our brain. What we are feeling is going to show up on our face. Are we feeling disgust, disapproval, or anger about the teen's pain or problem? Are we truly concerned and caring? Since pretending doesn't work well, we must at least be honest. We might have to be sure our RCs are on and then be sensitive to how and when we try to help. After a hurting or frustrated teen is calm and knows we care, then we can help them with alternative perspectives. Not in the form of a lecture, but as one adult to another.

Asking Forgiveness

As parents begin practicing joy-filled parenting with teens, the teens may open up and share how they have been hurt in the past by the parents.

This is a good sign and a great opportunity. Parents who can humbly ask forgiveness for their mistakes and failures will help their teen find healing from the hurts they've been carrying. There will be healing *with* their teens as well.

Lisa took Jason for Immanuel healing prayer and Jesus showed Jason some places from his childhood where he had felt very hurt and alone. As Jason worked through the memories, Lisa validated the memories. At the end of the prayer session, Lisa asked Jason to forgive her. He did and their connection grew.

Jason had a lot of courage to allow Jesus to take him back to times where he lacked validation and comfort that left him feeling upset and alone. Lisa had a lot of courage and humility to allow her teen to tell her how he had felt. When these kinds of hurts are left unresolved, they get triggered in the present. Like we saw in Shawnda's healing story, pain triggered in the present feels very true at that moment. It is very out of proportion to the present circumstance. Unresolved traumas and triggers are huge hindrances to joy-filled relationships. Humbly asking forgiveness at the right time helps restore the relationship.

Triggers

When triggered from an unresolved hurt, we do not realize the feelings are coming from the past. The emotions involved feel true in the present, but are out of proportion. When triggered we tend to blame the person in front of us when it might not be about them at all. As we learn to recognize triggers they can act as a red flag: here is something going on that needs healing! This is not about the person in front of me!

Getting healed and learning to suffer well instead of avoiding pain smooths the way for better relating between parents and teens. It's easier to stay relational. Heeding red flags stops the conflict. We are less likely to get overwhelmed. Turning to addictions to dull pain is not as attractive when we have joyful relationships, have taken our triggers to Jesus, and learned how to suffer well.

Taking our hurts to Jesus for healing shows us we are not alone because Jesus is, and always has been, with us. Like Jason, Lisa, John, and Shawnda we will walk in freedom from that old trigger. Teens will be relieved that we catch ourselves before conflict escalates. They will be glad that we don't turn on them in the present as we did before realizing triggers are from the past. When our triggers are healed, teens will benefit.

A while back I was able to help my teenage granddaughter, Rose, learn how to face and feel some unresolved pain in her life. In a later chapter I will elaborate on her story, but for now I want to share some background and one thing I did to help Rose learn that she didn't have to fear and avoid emotional pain. I helped her see that a benefit of emotional pain, when we re-frame it, is that it can show us how valuable we are. We don't hurt over worthless things. It's possible to turn painful negatives into positives because what causes us pain can tell us the characteristics of the heart that Jesus gave us. Here is a brief introduction to Rose's story and how she learned the characteristics of her heart.

Rose Needs Help

One day my son told me that Rose was struggling. He asked if I would talk to her. When I took her to lunch, she told me her eating disorder was back after being dormant for a couple of years. I realized that she was really hurting and there were more issues than just the eating. She was suicidal and dabbling in Pot. Things at home were not going well at all. She had a lot of anger.

As we talked I found out that Rose had been going to a counselor. When I asked if the counselor had asked her why she was acting out, she said, "No, Nana. No one is asking me why." This was upsetting to me because I believe that most acting out is because of unresolved pain; often unrecognized as a reason. We mistakenly focus on the "what" a teen is doing instead of the "why."

When avoiding pain, it's common to turn to other things to try to make the pain go away. These other things are not satisfying and don't last. I told Rose that I would come get her on Sunday and we could talk some more. I had an inkling that her unresolved pain was about a huge loss she had experienced when younger.

Working through Rose's struggles was very painful for everyone and took a few months. Her dad and mom were having their own pain, as they had to deal with the outbursts, the sneakiness, and the horror of what was going on. At first I was working with Rose by myself because from her perspective mom and dad were part of the problem. Later, we three adults got together on the same page.

Because I wanted to focus on the "why" of Rose's behavior, I took her to Jesus to show her the pain she was avoiding and for healing.[15] I used the Immanuel Prayer Approach for inner healing that Shawnda told us about earlier. Jesus met Rose and healed some old wounds. Later I helped Rose find the characteristics of her heart. This is one of the Tasks in the Adult Stage of maturity which you can see in Chapter Seven. We find the characteristics of our heart from what causes us pain. Knowing what causes us pain indicates a positive about the heart Jesus gave us. Finding the positive helps us learn to stop avoiding pain. Avoiding pain was what was causing Rose to act out. She did not know what to do with the pain from the unhealed wounds. I will share other skills I taught Rose later, but for now let's look at how to find a positive from our pain.

---

[15] *Share Immanuel* booklet, Wilder and Coursey, www.lifemodelworks.org and *The Immanuel Approach*, Dr. Karl Lehman, Immanuel Publishing, Evanston, IL, 2016; www.kclehman.com

Finding the Characteristics of One's Heart

With a partner, take turns telling your partner what hurts you. Use these questions:

- What causes me emotional pain? Come up with one or two words. (Examples: rejection, dishonesty, left out, disloyal. . .)

- What is something that I "get in trouble for" or am criticized for doing (not bad behavior)?

Brainstorm with your partner what the opposite of each pain that you share could be. **Write** down your opposites. Consider that these opposites are the main characteristics of your heart, and your partner's heart. **It is like you to hurt like this.** If time add other characteristics to each other's list. People love to be told the characteristics of their heart, even when it doesn't feel like it's true at first. Knowing our heart helps us suffer well because we know it's like us to hurt when these things are going on.

Rose discovered that it was like her to hurt when she had lost something important to her, when she was misunderstood, and/or when accused. The heart Jesus gave her is a connecting, kind, understanding, and loving heart.

CHAPTER SIX: RELATIONSHIPS ARE ABOUT RUPTURE AND REPAIR

Let's face it. Although we don't want to believe it's true, relationships are going to have ruptures, conflicts, and bumps. Most of us have learned to stuff them, ignore them, run away from them, or pretend they're not there. Many problems arise from these tactics. Nothing gets solved, brick-like walls keep people estranged, issues escalate, and everyone is miserable. Everyone hurts but pretends they don't. Teens are no different. They just behave like the models they see around them. What can we do about this common problem? Does God have an answer other than some commands in the Scripture about forgiving and being kind? Yes, He does. And it's actually designed into our brains.

Returning to Joy

We call God's design for repairing conflicts "returning to joy." Remember that Joy means *"someone is glad to be with me. I am the sparkle in someone's eye."* Joy is how our brains are designed to work and getting back to joy after conflict is part of the design.

Returning to joy means *"reconnecting with someone who hurt me."* It also means *staying connected and relational (heart open) during negative emotions.* In the last chapter, we already looked at how avoiding negative emotions causes addictions and other problems. Stuffing, ignoring, and pretending don't make negative emotions go away. Walking on eggshells is not a solution to prevent negative emotions. Marking people off who hurt us makes problems worse. Fear bonds abound. A better solution is to learn how to return to joy. When we have return-to-joy skills we are not as afraid of negative emotions because we know we will work out the problem. Knowing their family will work lovingly through problems is a gift to teens.

Six Negative Emotions

Ideally God designed the brain to learn return-to-joy around the age of twelve to eighteen months. There are six negative emotions from which we were supposed to learn paths in our brain back to joy. Those are anger, sad, fear, disgust, shame, and hopeless despair. If we did not learn a path back from one of these, we will avoid it (avoid pain) and go to a different emotion. Now we will see the problems we looked at earlier when avoiding pain—addictions, stuffing emotions, ruptures that don't get resolved, and controlling others through fear.

For this book I am not going to go deeply into the ins and outs of returning to joy, but there is greater detail in my books, *Joy-Filled Relationships* and *Re-Framing Your Hurts*. There is also a great little allegory by Denisia Huttula, *The Bridges of Chara,* which explains returning to joy in a story form.[16] For now we will just take a look at one of the emotions that seems to trip up a lot of people. Understanding this emotion and how to deal with it will help both parents and teens. Knowing how to handle it will set teens on a better path to relational maturity. That emotion is shame, a common, misunderstood cause of ruptures. By definition shame is difficult because it means *someone is* not *glad to be with me right now*. Shame is about correcting behavior *so we can* be glad to be together. Because most people have not been corrected correctly, shame has a bad name.

Two Kinds of Shame

Shame causes ruptures because correction has often been done in a condemning way; thus, we don't know how to handle shame as God designed it. And—we have not realized there are two kinds of shame. Just the word itself brings ugly feelings and connotations to our minds. Most of us upon hearing the word "shame" think about what is better called "toxic shame." Toxic shame is when correction is done incorrectly. The correction is about our personhood and communicates that we are bad. "You're a liar." "You're stupid." "You can't do anything right." "Why do you always mess up like that?" "I can't believe you did that!" "What's wrong with you?" These are just a few examples of toxic shame and all of us likely have plenty others of our own. Toxic shame is all about condemnation of identity. Condemnation can be communicated many

---

[16] *The Bridges of Chara* by Denisia Christine Huttula, amazon.com or openbench.com

different ways—verbally, non-verbally, facially—and it destroys a teen's heart.

Good shame is different. Good shame is hardwired into our brains by God. It's when someone is *not* glad to be with us, but unlike how we usually look at that, it's a good thing. It's about behavior. When given correctly, good shame is what helps us learn how to live with others, get along with others, and behave. Correction is necessary when behavior is off. Remember when we were talking about synchronizing in Chapter Three? We said that negative *behavior* needs correcting. Dr. Wilder says it this way, "We don't synchronize with naughty; we correct it."

The emphasis here for correcting is on behavior—not on personhood or feelings. Correction is given without condemnation of our teen's identity; we separate the two. Good shame emphasizes wanting to be close when some form of behavior is keeping us from being close—from being glad to be together. A good shame message communicates something like this: "I want to be close, but what you are doing keeps me from wanting to be close. Can we work on that so we can be close?"[17]

The problem that arises when someone has not learned what to do with shame is that regardless of how we sandwich our good shame message, they might still *hear* that they are bad. They just cannot take that there is *anything* wrong with them. Accusations, blaming, self-justifying, and defending immediately come flying back at the messenger—or from those with a quieter side—pouting and withdrawing.

Here is an example of someone hearing toxic shame when the messenger was giving a good shame message: Luke laughed and made a joke about his daughter's new hairdo. When he looked across the table at his wife, she was not laughing. He inquired as to what was wrong. She stated softly that she didn't want to take part in putting someone down. Luke got angry and accused her of saying he was a bad father. His wife had said nothing like that. Luke "heard" toxic shame because of his own

---

[17] Learned from Dr. Wilder personally.

lack of knowing what to do with correction. He needs a path back to joy from shame.

Giving Good Shame Messages

Humility is a big factor in learning back-to-joy from shame. We have to be willing to admit our failures and mistakes instead of getting defensive when someone gives us a good shame message. Admitting mistakes is easier when we feel safe and likely won't be condemned. The good shame messenger helps us practice receiving the good shame by their voice tone and kind words. We need to keep in mind how to give correcting messages as we help our teens learn to receive them better. The Bible calls saying something that needs to be said, "Speaking the truth in love." (Ephesians 4:15).

We might wonder why Dr. Wilder uses different words such as, "good shame messages?" Why doesn't he just say, "Speak the truth in love?" The answer to that question is one reason this material is so effective. Dr. Wilder's "strange" lingo is purposeful—it makes us think. When we hear familiar words that we've heard a thousand times, we dismiss them thinking we know how to walk them out. I have found very few people who give good shame messages—and even fewer who can receive good shame messages.

Receiving Good Shame Messages

A friend asked me recently to give an example of receiving a good shame message. That reminded me of a time when my daughter and I were doing a project and she said to me, "You're hurrying me." She just stated it without unkindness. It did not bother me at all and that surprised me for a second. Then I realized that my brain had learned a better path back from good shame. In the past I likely would have had hurt feelings. Another friend was helping me on the computer and I was chatting. She stated that she couldn't talk with me while working on the computer. Again I was not bothered; I was encouraged to see how I had grown.

When we or our teens do not know what to do with shame, problems arise and blossom. Blaming, self-justifying, pouting, attacking, or turning it around do not enhance relationships; they're all ways to avoid shame. Not diminishing the importance of the other five negative emotions, we desperately need to learn how to handle shame. We all have to learn that good shame is necessary, that it's OK, and how to give and receive it. Our teens need to know they are loved and wanted even when corrected.

Here is an interesting tip: We need to allow our teens to correct *us* with good shame messages. Teens love to feel the power of being honest with a humble, kind parent. As we all learn, it will take promptings from God to remain humble. Along the way we will need a loving family or community to help us learn how to handle all of our negative emotions and return to joy.

Lisa and John handled a conflict well after a correction and everyone returned to joy.

Lisa and John Repair a Rupture

Last night Jason was playing a podcast on his laptop in the common area after we had agreed to be sensitive to others about sound. I asked him to put it in his ears (using earphones) since we were trying to relax for bedtime. He reacted to my request almost enraged, and said, "I'm listening to a sermon!" He started arguing like he used to do before we started Joy-Filled Relationships and had a tone of disrespect and disgust. I could see his reaction was out of proportion to the "offense," which I am learning is a sign of him being triggered.

Feeling a need for help in applying the joy-filled principles, I called John to join me as we tried to stay relational and engage with Jason's heart rather than punish him for his tone. We used words at first to explain ourselves, but then remembered we learned that when someone is triggered and melted down they don't hear any words. So in the midst of the escalating moment, I pulled out my tool of synchronizing. I zipped my mouth and just looked at Jason with a joy smile and gave his hand an appropriate touch. He started melting, but then chose to be un-relational again and walked off, growling "Akkkk!"

In the past I would have followed him and told him he lost his phone for a period of time, or spoken unhelpful words with an unintentional judging tone. Instead we let him cool off. Before bed, John asked him if he would be willing to synchronize and build joy with us. Because he has had such a positive experience with feeling loved by doing this in the past with us, he agreed. We sat on the floor and each took a turn synchronizing eye-to-eye with him and then gave him a hug. In the past I would have brought up the conflict again to get the last word in or bring unnecessary closure making sure he knows he understands my point of view. Instead, I chose to stay relational and we all went to bed feeling loved and connected. Later when I told this story to Barbara, she reminded me to ignore the growls that came after a confrontation. Teens are saving face with their, "Akkkkk!" or "Whatever!!??" Just ignore it.

This story from John and Lisa illustrates both of the definitions for returning to joy that we looked at earlier. Let's look at the two angles separately in some similar scenarios that also illustrate return-to-joy.

Two Angles

Our definition of return-to-joy had two angles: 1) Reconnecting with someone who hurt us. 2) Being glad to be together *during* strong emotions. First let's look at a scenario when we've had a conflict and need to reconnect with someone. Keep in mind that there are many factors that affect how a conflict plays out, such as maturity, skill levels, and intensity of the emotions. Let's consider times that are more or less usual for families living and working together. How can we handle conflicts in a relational manner and return to joy?

Here is a summary of the "steps" that might help, followed by examples and scenarios:

1. Disengage to calm down if needed.

2. Make certain at least the parent's Relational Circuits are on.

3. Share the distress and be glad to be together regardless of the emotions.

4. Validate and Comfort if appropriate.

5. Model what it's like us to do in this emotion. (This does not mean a lecture on feeling different.)

6. Separate behavior and identity if correcting.

Conflicts can be handled relationally by "practicing the pause" and getting Relational Circuits on before any discussion. (See Chapter Two.) We cannot solve any problem with Relational Circuits off. In order to return to joy, at least one person needs to be acting like him or herself. Someone has to synchronize and see the other's perspective. (Chapter Three) Of course this takes some maturity, so if both parent and teen lack maturity at the moment, repair will be difficult, and maybe even impossible, until later. It is absolutely vital to have the RCs on.

For the sake of our discussion let's say the parent is able to stay calm and relational and act like him or herself. He or she may have to disengage first and go aside to calm down and get the RCs on. Disengaging to calm is not the same as running way, withdrawing, or putting up a wall. With the RCs on we are better able to validate the feelings and communicate calmly that we want to be together and work things out. If the teen responds somewhat calmly, we can move towards a two-way discussion. Parent and teen can listen and re-state the other's perspective.

Calm tones are extremely important with no hint of accusing, nagging, or correcting from the parent. Always separate identity from behavior. Condemnation makes things worse. *The more mature person will model what it's like us to do (what God says to do) during this emotion. The modeling is principally non-verbal.* (Not a lecture) At times, instructions may work when everyone is calm and ready to listen.

The second scenario has similarities, but this time it's not about conflict so much as it's about being glad to be with someone having an emotion from which they don't know how to get back to joy. There might be fear during a scary circumstance. A teen might feel sad because of a loss. Maybe he or she feels angry because of how a situation was handled. Perhaps they don't know how to respond to correction. When we are not part of the problem that our teen is upset about, we can help if we know how to get back from that emotion. *We share the distress (synchronize) and be glad to be together while the teen's brain watches (absorbs) how we handle the emotion. Validation and comfort help. They will feel comforted and understood. Over time, they will develop that place in their brain to return to joy from that emotion.* Go back and note in Lisa's story where she and John did most of the return-to-joy skills.

Being in Joy Groups where people are learning and practicing these skills also helps us learn because the group is a safe place to share how we are feeling. As we listen to others' stories about how they are applying the material, we learn from their examples. Learning to return to joy, whether at twelve to eighteen months or later is all done non-verbally. We learn these skills from others who know them and are glad to be with us *during the emotion as they model non-verbally what it is like us to do when feeling it.* We can teach this information to those who don't know it, but the skills cannot be learned from a book.[18] (See the book, *Transforming Fellowship* for details on all of the nineteen skills.)

Lisa has another great story that illustrates the application of return-to-joy. After some months of doing very little correcting as they sought to re-build the lost relationships with Jason and Jonathan, there came a time when they felt the need to address some anger.

---

[18] *Transforming Fellowship* by Chris M. Coursey. www.lifemodelworks.org

Dealing with Anger Relationally

When our now 18 year old son, Jason, was little and began expressing anger, I didn't know about the brain science and the importance of joy filled relationships. I thought that the most important thing to do as a parent was to give him consequences so that he would behave obediently. When he started to have a meltdown during a home school group I was leading, I picked him up, feeling angry myself about his interruption of my class. I carried him upstairs and put him in his room. I spoke sternly to him and told him not to come back downstairs until he stopped crying.

Now I cringe at telling that story because I see how my failure to synchronize with him and stay relational has affected my son and kept him from growing in emotional maturity. As a result, he has never developed the ability to return to joy from anger. Now that we are learning the JFP brain skills, we have been helping Jason learn this Infant Stage skill.

The other night he was angry at me and I called my husband in to help me stay relational. The conversation started going down that old path and finally I remembered how to synchronize with him. I gave an appropriate touch to his arm, zipped my mouth and I matched his facial expression, intensity and tone through my eyes. I saw him start to cool down. The arguing ended and he went to his room, probably for a break.

Later, John and I asked if he would like to build joy (eye-to-eye) again and he agreed. Before bed, we each took a turn looking into his eyes and feeling delight for him. We spoke no words, but thought loving thoughts that communicated non-verbally. We hugged and were all connected and feeling joy again. It was not necessary to revisit the issue of Jason's anger. We knew he understood what we expected from him and he had had plenty of opportunity to voice his disagreement to us. John and I continued to hold the line with the behavior we had been discussing with him.

Because Jason had not learned what it's like us to do when angry, Lisa and John allowed him to feel what he needed to feel, then they modeled non-verbally how to return to joy by staying glad to be with him in the anger. There was no need to continue lecturing Jason about the situation. He knew he needed to follow the guideline that brought up the discussion. But as they worked through it, he felt understood. He felt accepted. And he felt loved. Thinking later about the story, we realized that John had helped Lisa return to joy from fear when he came to help. Lisa was able to get her Relational Circuits back on and remember what it was like her to do to help Jason. Again note which skills they applied.

CHAPTER SEVEN: WE ARE RAISING ADULTS

Now that we have looked at a few topics around emotional maturity, learning to suffer well, and returning to joy, let's take a look at the maturity stages developed at Life Model Works which we mentioned earlier in Chapter Four. I learned about these stages many years ago from Dr. Wilder of Life Model Works (LMW). I see these stages as a vital part of parenting and growth.

Around the age of thirteen, children are entering the Adult stage of life and this brings big changes for parents and new teens. Many parents are not aware of the Infant and Child Needs and Tasks that came before the Adult stage, nor are they aware of what comes in the Adult stage. The following comprehensive, practical lists can help parents see what is missing from everyone's earlier years. The lists are a road map for teens to know what needs to be learned from thirteen to the birth of the first child before entering the Parent Stage.

If parents have not been aware of these Needs and Tasks, there's no worry. We don't want to feel overwhelmed by what's missing. With time and patience we can fill in some of the holes. It will be good and necessary for parents to look at the Needs and Tasks for themselves since we can only take our children through the level we ourselves have reached.

These stages (and the two not shown here) are copyrighted. The questions in parentheses are mine for clarification.

THE STAGES

Dr. E. John Wilder/Questions by Barbara Moon

All rights reserved by Life Model Works

THE INFANT STAGE   **Ideal Age: Birth to Age 4**

Infant Needs

1. Joy Bonds with both parents that are strong, loving, caring, secure

    (Did I (and my children) have a loving caring secure bond with each parent? What if my bonds were fear based? If so, do I **now** have a loving caring bond with a woman?   Do I have one with a man?)

2. Important needs are met without asking

    (Were my needs (and my children's) met in these first 3-4 years without me asking? One has to receive before giving. The adults met my needs instead of me being the "parent." If it was reversed, how have I dealt with that?)

3. Quiet together time

    (Do I (and my children) know how to quiet myself? Do I regularly have quiet together with   another person? With God? (This is quietness inside, not just sitting still.))

4. Help regulating distressing emotions

    (How am I (and my children) doing with the Big Six emotions? (See chapter on rupture and repair.))

5. Be seen through the "eyes of Heaven"

    (Do I (and my children) know I am accepted and loved outside of my behavior? Do I accept myself based on Heaven's eyes? Do I have at least one person who sees me this way?)

6. Receive and give life

    (Can I (and my children) receive without guilt or shame? Do I think I have to "give all the time?" Can I do good things for myself without feeling guilty?)

7. Have others synchronize with him/her first

    (Can I (and my children) allow another to help me, comfort me and synchronize with me without feeling guilt or shame? {Comforting a crying baby teaches hope.})

Infant Tasks

1. Receive with joy

    (Can I (and my children) receive with joy without feeling guilty or refusing the gesture? Do I try to keep others from serving me, helping me? Am I able to just say "thank you?")

2. Learn to synchronize with others

    (Am I (and my children) learning to synchronize (be in tune with) with others of all ages?)

3. Organize self into a person through imitation

    (Babies learn who they are by imitation, not instructions. Whoever pays attention to them is the one(s) they model after in these years. The attention can be positive or negative. They go by the face and what they see there to determine their worth and identity. Their cries are asking for help to feel better.)

    (Do I (and my children) know who I am as a person? What is like me? Whom did I imitate growing up? What was my principle caretaker like? Have I had or do I have someone in my life now to help me form an identity or improve it?)

4. Learn to regulate emotion

    (Baby learns to regulate by being allowed to rest before she is overwhelmed. Mother synchronizes and knows when to allow rest during the joy building.)

5. Learn to return to joy from every emotion

    (Can I (and my children) be myself when upset in all the emotions? Which ones am I (my child) good at, which am I lacking? How do I (my child) handle disappointment and humiliation?)

6. Learn to be the same person over time

    (Am I (and my children) the same person when upset as when I am in joy? Would others say I am moody and different when angry or upset? Do I have someone to help me learn the missing skills?)

7. Learn self-care skills

    (Am I (and my children) able to take care of myself? At this stage, just myself is enough. As an adult that might mean saying "no" to things or asking for help when needed.)

8. Learn to rest

    (Can I (and my children) rest and not be hyper or intense all the time? This means inside rest as well as outside. Am I willing to learn this and do I have someone to help me with it?)

THE CHILD STAGE   **Ideal Age: Ages 4-13**

I have taken some of my comments here from *Living With Men*, by Dr. John Wilder. www.lifemodelworks.org At this age, the child will begin to branch out more into "daddy's world." He will begin to venture further from mom than before, growing into some independence, knowing mom is there for reassurance and help. Mom will no longer guess at the needs, the child will begin to ask and receive. If the child has had a close bond, he or she will know that when bad things happen it brings comfort. He doesn't have to fear adversity and pain. He knows there is a path back to joy. He does not have to control others to get needs met. He knows how to use his words.

Child Needs

1. Weaning

    (Weaning is the end of infancy and only done well by well-trained four year old brains. If the child was raised on fear, weaning will not go well. He or she will not know their needs and feelings.)

    (Have I healthily separated from my mother? Do I (my child) expect people to read my mind? Can I take care of myself? What kind of relationship did I have with my father? Did he respond positively to my requests for needs? Did he show me how to increasingly take care of myself and broaden my world? Did I learn to go out on "adventures" and return home to rest?)

2. Help to do what he does not feel like doing

    (Can I (and my children) do things I do not feel like doing? Do I understand that others do not *only* do what they feel like doing? This skill learned around the age of five prepares us to be able to do hard things.)

3. Help sorting feelings, imaginations and reality.

    (Can I (and my children) separate feelings, imaginations and reality? Do I understand how the "real world" operates? Do I know how to judge if my feelings are real or not? Do I believe everything I feel? Do I have someone in my life that I can trust to tell me the truth and help me change my understanding when I have a misconception?)

4. Feedback on guesses, attempts and failures

   (Have I (and my children) been allowed to learn through my mistakes without being overly punished or rejected? Am I confident to take appropriate risks or am I overly performance based?)

5. Be taught the family history

   (Do I (and my children) know how my family came to be? This comes around the age of twelve. Was I taught how my actions would affect history? Did I hear stories of my family history? Was I taught how to avoid continuing the negative parts of my family history?)

6. Be taught the history of God's family

   (Do I (and my children) know the story of God's family? Was I taught how to truly live by knowing the stories and people of the One who gives life and knows how to do it? If not, am I learning that now?)

7. Be taught the "big picture" of life

   (Do I (and my children) understand the big picture of life? Do I understand consequences of my behavior can affect generations? Did I learn that I am not entitled to things without working? Was I prepared to become an adult by having a map that showed the path to maturity?)

Child Tasks

1. Take care of self (one is enough right now)

   (Do I know how to take care of myself by saying, "No," when necessary? Did I receive love that I did not have to earn? Can I look back and notice any of the identity changes I have gone through? Did I have to take care of someone else when too young?)

2. Learn to ask for what he/she needs

   (Do I (and my children) know how to ask for what I need? I do not expect others to read my mind and guess what I need? I can ask without feeling guilty. (Unmet needs produce anger.))

3. Learn self-expression

   (Am I (and my children) able to enjoy myself without feeling guilty or inhibited? Can I express myself and not have to have someone else talk for me?)

4. Develop personal resources and talents

   (Am I (and my children) growing at what I am good at? Do I know my talents and spiritual gifts?)

5. Learn to make himself/herself understandable to others

   (If someone misunderstands me, do I (and my children) try in a calm way to help him or her understand me?)

6. Learn to do hard things

   (I (and my children) know how to do hard things. This is more than just getting up to go to work. It is also emotionally hard things—like facing pain and not avoiding it. I can actually choose to do hard things even if they hurt.)

7. Learn what satisfies

   (I (and my children) know what satisfies. Satisfaction has a 24-hour shelf life, so it needs to be renewed each day. Some things that satisfy are sharing joy, doing hard things and getting through them, receiving and giving life, food, love, efforts. I know I am entitled to have my needs met. I receive joyfully, but also give cheerfully so as not to be only a consumer. I was not expected to sacrificially give before I was mature enough. (Ecclesiastes 8:15))

8. Tame the *nucleus accumbens (the pleasure center in the brain)*—our cravings

   (Have I (and my children) tamed my cravings? (Genesis 25: 27-32) or I am working on that and have someone to help me and keep me accountable? If I have addictions, am I admitting and getting help?)

9. See self through the "eyes of Heaven"

   (I (and my children) see myself through Heaven's eyes because someone else has seen or is seeing me that way. I am at least learning how God looks at me.)

THE ADULT STAGE   Ideal Age: Age 13-first child

(If your child is over age 13, insert his/her name also)

Adult Needs

1. A rite of passage

   (Do I remember any kind of "rite of passage" as I became a teen? What might we as a family like to do for our children as they become this age?[19] Was I prepared well for becoming an adult?)

2. Time to bond with peers and form a group identity

   (How did I progress through my teen years? Was I allowed to form a group identity? Did I choose a group that was a good or a bad influence? Did my community help me with a group identity? Am I allowing my teen to form a healthy group identity?)

---

[19] For good tips on rite of passage for boys see *On Ramp: Helping Your Son On His Journey to Manhood* by Bob Moon, amazon.com

3. Inclusion by the same-sex community

    (Did I have community with other men or women growing up? Do I have community with other men or women now? Do I feel included? Does my teen?)

4. Observing the same sex using their power fairly

    (Can I use my power fairly? Do I know how to negotiate and compromise? Have I seen this modeled by other men or women? Has my teen?)

5. Being given important tasks by his/her community

    (Was I given important tasks growing up? Do I feel I have an important place in my community now? (The Mormons do this with their young men who are required to serve 2 years. What is the main ingredient needed when we give young people an important task? We have to TRUST them. What if they fail? Jesus trusted the untrustworthy without condemning their failures.)

6. Guidance for the personal imprint they will make on history

    (Do I realize that because I am alive, life will not be the same for other people? Was I told how my behavior could affect history? Do I and my teen understand that now? *(The movie, It's a Wonderful Life is an example of this))*

7. Opportunities to share life in partnership

    (Have I had opportunities to share life in partnership? Have I practiced being in partnership with peers and older adults? Does my teen have these kinds of opportunities?)

Adult Tasks

1. Take care of two of more at the same time

    (Am I able to take emotional and physical care of two or more at the same time? Can I negotiate and compromise so that all are satisfied?

Do I understand the real meaning of fairness? Is my teen learning this? (A good analogy—A real estate agent's main job is to discover what everyone needs and bring all to satisfaction in the negotiations.))

2. Discover the main characteristics of his/her heart

    (Do I know the main characteristics of my heart? Do I know what hurts me and how that pain shows me the characteristics of my heart? Have I had or do I have someone who tells me the truth about my heart, encouraging me and supporting me as I live with a heart like mine and the pain it can bring? Do I know the spiritual disciplines that help me take care of my heart? Does my teen know these things?)

3. Proclaim and defend personal and community(group) identity

    (Can I tell others who I am and who my community is? Does my teen know what it's like us to do as God's family? Cults and gangs do this. Christianity calls it evangelism—telling the Good News.)

4. Bring self and others back to joy simultaneously

    (Can I bring myself and others back to joy (reconnect) at the same time. Do I maintain who I am and act like myself when distress and conflict come? Adults realize, "We can do this together." Is my teen learning these skills? Can I be glad to be with those in the shadows by being with them where they are? Are others glad to be with the "real me" or someone I want them to think I am? Do I have any relationships that are estranged and need repair? (This does not include unsafe relationships))

5. Develop a personal style that reflects his/her heart

    (Do I/ my teen have personal style that reflects the uniqueness of my/his/her heart?)

6. Learn to protect others from himself/herself

   (Do I protect others from myself by removing myself when not able to stay calm and act like myself? Do I manipulate to get my own way? Am I able to interact without overwhelming another? Do I notice when someone says, "ouch!" Do I ask forgiveness when I hurt others? How is my teen doing learning these skills? *(It is very important to recognize that something hurts. Many have avoided or repressed pain or been taught that it is not okay to know/admit that something hurts—for reasons such as, others may not care, no comfort, no support, codependency, etc. We have to say it hurts when it hurts.))*

7. Learn to diversify and blend roles

   (Can I function healthily and with balance in various roles that I am called to do?)

8. Life-giving sexuality

   (Do I/my teen know what it means to have life-giving sexuality? Have I had healing and/or redemption of any non-life-giving sexuality from my past? Do I understand why God has instructions about this area of life?)

9. Mutual satisfaction in a relationship

   (Do I know how to find a compromise that will satisfy both people in a relationship? Do I have to always win? Do I know how to share and use my power wisely? *(Some ways to share power with children are things such as allowing them to have a say so about their rooms, helping them achieve goals, not being overly strict, allowing failures and mistakes, allowing age appropriate decisions.))*

10. Partnership

(Partnership in marriage (and other relationships) is like buddy breathing on a deep-sea dive. It is like working out on many different machines at the gym in order to develop different muscles. (p. 116 LWM)[20]

Importance of the Adult Stage

Now that we have seen the first three of the Maturity Stages, we can see the important task before us in parenting teens. Moving into the Adult Stage brings a whole new approach for relating to our teen. A big change will be that a teen's focus will be less at home and more on peers as they form a group identity. Forming a group identity is vital to maturity. Teens who get stuck in the Child Stage and don't form a healthy group identity become narcissistic and carry immaturity into their relationships and marriages. This crucial time is part of parents letting go so that their teens can move into building their group identity and towards becoming their own person. We will look at the need for letting go in more detail later.

So many other important tasks are part of the Adult Stage. In the coming years the teens will need to learn how to take care of more than one person at a time and achieve mutual satisfaction in a relationship. (Remember Lisa's story about showing her boys how to learn mutual satisfaction?) Teens will need to feel important in their community. How are they serving others in need? Are they able to do important tasks at church or school? Are teens included in family decisions?

Teens need to move towards being able to bring others back to joy simultaneously, a skill that involves togetherness. As they grow in strength and encounter more and more stress, they have to know how to protect others from themselves. This means to disengage and calm down before hurting someone. It's important to be gentle responders, patient

---

[20] I have not listed the Parent or Elder stages here. The principle attribute of the parent stage is that a parent gives without expecting anything in return. The Elder is ready to help take care of his or her community. For more on the Maturity Stages see my book, *Joy-Filled Relationships,* and *Living with Men* by Dr. Wilder.

with weakness. And teens must know how their choices affect history and understand the "big picture" of life.

Reading through these aspects of the Adult Stage, being reminded of the tasks that teens and young adults will need to accomplish in order to mature, it's easy to feel overwhelmed—and even more so when we realize that we parents are guides along the way. What I desire to do here is at least lighten our load somewhat, as we look at a few points that can help us relate a bit differently while moving through the teen and young adult years. I want to share some points that I found helpful with my own concerns as the parent of teenagers. Now I'm a grandparent and I've applied these guides to my grandchildren. Some of the concerns and questions I had with my teens have changed over the years while some remain the same. But most of all, I want to encourage us to trust God and walk with Him through every phase and trial that comes with having a teenager. Shawnda will have several stories, so stick with us as we expand on the changes during these years.

CHAPTER EIGHT: HOW DOES MY PARENTING CHANGE?

Some of us have been interested in good parenting skills since our kids were born. Nothing motivates more than holding a brand new baby and feeling that rush of overwhelming love for this precious one that we have so longed for. Perhaps we adopted and the child was a bit older. No matter, our heart swells with love and wonder just the same. The years pass and parenting becomes a little more difficult. Conflicts, trials, discipline, and worries are woven throughout the years. We hear others talk about the teen years and we dread even getting to middle school. Never fear. Delight, wonder, love, and joy can abound in the teen years as well. But there will have to be some changes—some big changes. Those changes can be frightening as control slips more and more through our fingers. Here is a story from Shawnda about how she tried to control something Trey was doing before she knew joy-filled teen parenting—and how it didn't work.

A Battle Lost

Before I learned joy-filled relationships it was easy for me to try to control Trey. Trey often played a video game that I really hated. It was centered around sorcery and evil and magic and just didn't sit well with me. I must have talked to him a dozen times about it to no avail. One day I had this awesome idea—or so I thought. I told him I would buy the game from him and he could go to the store and buy a new one with the money! A great idea! Right? Wrong. He did take me up on the offer, and bought a different game. But—not too much longer after that he went back to the store and bought the exact same game again! Ugh! Battle lost.

This is an example of my ideas before learning about joy and relationships. I approached dealing with Trey from the perspective that the problem is bigger than the relationship instead of the other way around. Eventually the games lost their influence over Trey when he began to see on his own that video games were not the way to experience true risk and adventure. Being an Eagle Scout and an outdoorsman helped him see that he was wasting time on the games and not living life to the fullest. Real life adventures were a lot better. I lost this battle, but I did learn from it.

This story makes me laugh. Don't we try so hard to get our teens to see our perspective? I see God's sense of humor as well when He lets us go for it and it doesn't work. Then He does more in a moment than we can in days.

Trusting Instead of Hovering

When kids are small we feel that we have a sense of control because we are with them, or know who is with them, most of the time. We screen play-dates and sleep-overs as if they were going to work for the CIA. We trust our schools and families. Now we have a teenager who wants to be with friends more than anyone else. And Heaven help us, they can drive. So we must find a good balance between our "hovering" and knowing everything to a place of trusting. Hovering means we are trying to control something that's impossible to control—everything about another person. Hovering is the opposite of what teens need. Letting go of control and trusting both the teen and God is going to keep us on our knees.

In the next chapter we will look at some tips for troubled teens, but for now let's look at some normal transitions needed as our child moves into the teen years. There will be times that we have to trust our teens in spite of how it feels and even how things appear. It's helpful not to jump to conclusions. It's important not to attack or accuse. When parents accuse teens of negative behavior that they are not doing, it is very painful. Sometimes accusing pushes a teen towards doing something they would not have done.

I know one mom who took this to heart and saved herself a big mess. The son was not answering his phone at an hour that he was supposed to be in contact. Mom imagined all kinds of scenarios and her anger grew. She remembered that accusing was not helpful so she waited until she picked her son up. He was where he had said he would be, but he was in the pool without the phone. If she had jumped on him for lack of contact, it would have been very hurtful to him. She was very glad she had waited to hear his explanation. Of course there are times when situations have to be spoken to, but with teens we are going to do less correcting, no nagging, and more letting go of control.

Not only will it be helpful to trust more and hover less, there needs to be a change in our approach to school work and chores. If we have been involved in homework, it's time to wean teens from our help as much as possible. Being in charge of their school work will prepare them for college and/or the real world where they have to keep up their responsibilities without a lot of help. Chores are not a hill to die on if nagging is needed.

Treat as Adults

As teens move into high school and into young adult hood, if they are still at home (or home from college) we are going to begin to treat them as we would another adult. Some sharing of household chores is part of being an adult, but how we try to get others to help can cause unnecessary conflict. Shawnda decided not to nag her young adult son about chores. She sensed Jesus telling her to approach Trey a different way. He began to do more voluntarily.

Your Part

My husband and I are coming close to having an empty nest. We are somewhat getting used to doing all of the cleaning in the house on our own with no army to shout orders to. We planned on cleaning one Saturday morning and Trey had planned to leave early and go do some errands. My normal is to ask him to help with the cleaning, but mid-sentence of my request for help I said to him, "No. We don't need help; we just need you to do your part before you go." In my head I thought, "Hmm…that's a new thought!" He responded with an OK and did clean his room and bathroom and did some vacuuming.

Here's the kicker though—I did not tell him what his part was! He made his own choices about it and I thanked him for taking the time and for his good effort. This was an amazing milestone for us.

One of the important things I got out of this incident is something big to really grab hold of—being satisfied with even the smallest amount of effort. At another time, not right then, you discuss some of what your ideas are for the teen's part of cleaning. You must resist the desire to make a list and to make your agenda more important than the relationship! If we continue in the pattern of suggesting everything to Trey, he will never see on his own what needs to be done.

I was so grateful for this lesson in patience and satisfaction. It is now how we approach all our adult children conversations. It's important for us all to remember that effort looks different every time it's given. Your teen's effort looks different than your effort. Your effort can look different every day as well.

Relating well with our teens is very satisfying and noticing efforts instead of lacks is an excellent way to promote good will. We feel satisfaction as we watch them grow and change. They feel satisfied because they were not nagged or belittled as we help them move through the Adult Stage.

Here is another great story from Shawnda that I wish readers could hear her tell in person. We lose something here when we can't see the expressions on her face when she relates how this story took place. This is one of my favorites.

A Cigar Story

A year or so ago I was walking into our kitchen while Trey was making a sandwich at the island. Before I had a chance to even say hello, he held up a cigar and said, "Oh by the way, this is mine." I had been practicing the pause before I spoke to him, so I paused as my chin dropped and my eyes widened, then stuttered out, "Uh, why?" He said he wanted to try it and that the guys at the shop would sometimes smoke cigars at break time. While there were many things for me to say at that moment, I mostly just issued health warnings and dental issues and said thank you for telling me.

Later, during an Immanuel prayer moment I asked Jesus what He wanted me to know about Trey smoking a cigar? Jesus spoke clearly, "Tell Trey to smoke with Me." What!? I left my shock there and I didn't ask Jesus anything else at that moment. I went about my day pondering what He had said.

Later it seemed clear to me that His desire was that I let Him take care of this and not dwell on it. I told my husband and when I saw Trey that evening I told him what Jesus had said. Trey smiled, bowed his head a bit, and said, "OK, I'll do that."

It amazes me that when I let Jesus handle something big like this, how it can be peaceful and full of grace. Since I didn't blow up and deliver a bunch of angry rules, the cigar smoking did not become something Trey had to fight about. It had no control over him. No bondage to sin and rebellion took place. He was able to bow his head at the words of Jesus and not be stiff-necked about it. He says he has smoked occasionally since then, but I am so happy to say that it is not a regular occurrence in his life.

Smoking a cigar may not be one of the worst things we could encounter, but Shawnda gets the point across well. Her reaction was one that did not make things worse. She trusted Jesus to handle it and Trey could try his wings. Shawnda focused on Trey's heart and kept in mind that teens and young adults are supposed to individuate and become their own person. (We will look at individuation in a later chapter.)

Helpful Words

When we do encounter a problem with our teens, a good way to practice seeing their heart is to remember to use words something like these: "You aren't acting like yourself right now. What's going on? How can I help?" These words help teens feel more understood and less corrected or attacked. Shawnda tried this out with Trey and it worked beautifully.

Messy Bedroom

Trey really likes his room to be neat and clean. He prefers a minimalist approach. This has been his way of keeping his room since he was very young. I walked in his room one day to take him something and it was quite a mess! Clothes were everywhere and the bed unmade. It occurred to me that something must be amiss. Normally I would have fussed at him, but this time I said "Hey buddy, what's up? It's not like you to have a mess like this. Is there anything going on? Anything I can help with?"

He was open to talk about being overwhelmed with some things going on and even how he was stuck on making some decisions. He appreciated that I asked how he was doing. Considering that my relationship with him is more important than the problem of a messy bedroom created a deeper relationship between us. He felt known and loved which helped him to get unstuck.

After our talk, I responded to his "weakness" with gentle support by cleaning his bathroom and doing his laundry to help him get caught up. A messy bedroom might be the norm for your teen, but the principle is the same—notice what seems "off" and instead of fussing, check why they are not acting like themselves.

Noticing that our teen is not acting like him or herself instead of correcting or fussing at them takes the edge off of our bumps. It feels more caring and affirms identity. It lessens the likelihood of getting defensive. It gives us an opportunity to model the new skills and leaves a door open for dialogue.

As we introduce these new relational skills into the family, it's good to practice them patiently. If spending quality time with a teen has not been normal or frequent, when possible begin taking the teen out to lunch or a movie, something that interests them. It's important for parents to show interest in what their teen likes, even if it's boring to the parent. One of the best tips I've heard from Shawnda was when she told us that Jesus had shown her something to do when Trey wanted to talk about trucks and engines. We saw that story in Chapter Two, but I want to repeat part of it here because it's so life-changing.

Picturing

While Trey was talking to me about trucks and engines, I would synchronize my face with his, whether it was happy or intense or frustrated. This helped me to stay in the present and be engaged without leaving him feeling as if I wasn't interested. I also pictured Trey as he was around the age of four, cute and adorable. I believe these good thoughts showed up on my face.

Remember back in the chapters about brain development where we talked about an infant becoming like the faces he beholds? Shawnda's story reminds us that it remains just as important during the teen and adult years. None of us ever get over needing to be seen "through Heaven's eyes." Teens learn a "new" (older) identity from the faces which are around them now. Faces communicate whether we are glad, or not glad, to be with someone. This is what Lisa referred to in her return-to-joy from anger story with Jason. She and John think good thoughts and delightful memories when they synchronize and build joy with their teens. It's all non-verbal, showing up in eyes and on faces. And these parents are finding that joy works.

Acceptance and Listening

Shawnda's story of seeing Trey as his cute little four year old self reminds us how important it is to accept and listen to our teens. People of all ages thrive on acceptance. Now your teen needs unconditional acceptance even more than ever, as he or she tries their wings and moves towards becoming an independent person. It's important to support them as they branch out and try new things. As we practice joy skills, we might find ourselves looking at a situation differently than we thought we would. Here is a story from Lisa that illustrates her change of attitude:

Camping and Cooking

Jonathan was going on a student leadership retreat with 11 others and he told me he and his friend were "volunteered" to plan and cook dinner. I was frustrated because, since Jonathan doesn't cook, it felt as though I was the one volunteered. I also quickly assumed that meant I was paying for the meal as well. He asked me to take him to the store after school. There was no meal plan...his plan was to wing it. I was a bit angry about the whole lack of planning and uncertainty about the financial commitment. My gut reaction was to say, "No." I thought that would force the rest of the students to share the responsibility and teach Jonathan not to let people volunteer him and me for things.

After reaching out for advice and considering Joy-Filled Parenting, I decided instead to take him to the store. My new perspective was that my relationship with my son was more important than the problem of my inconvenience. This enabled me to view planning and cooking a meal for his fellow students as a life skill that would be great for him to learn. As a highly social teen his future would likely be full of opportunities to plan and cook meals for groups.

Valuing the relationship made me realize that training my son in this skill was more important than teaching him a lesson on saying no to pushy people. It would not be worth making him feel unsupported and potentially alone in the awkwardness of going back to the group and saying no. We sat down together and I helped him brainstorm meal ideas and things to consider when cooking for a group of 12. He made a grocery list and his leader actually ended up doing the shopping. It ended up being a wonderful experience between us, one of bonding and joy, as we worked on this project together. I was so thankful I chose to value his heart rather than what I thought was unfair in the situation.

Again we see how Lisa's courage to ask for advice and look at her teen's heart completely turned a situation upside down. Seeing God's perspective helps us change ours.

Our ability to unconditionally accept our children gets fine-tuned as our teens grow up, because how and what they choose and how they change may not line up exactly as we had hoped. Some differences may be mild and some may bring us grief. Whatever the case, regardless of our feelings, it's imperative to accept and love our teen no matter the behavior, the characteristics, or the beliefs. We may not agree with them and their choices, but our love does not change.

Listening and not lecturing are vital to accepting a teen in spite of behavior and beliefs. We continue to synchronize throughout life, regardless of age. Teens want to be with people who synchronize and try to understand them. Nagging and lecturing do not help anyone. In this chapter we are looking at things that change. Treating our teens somewhat as we would a friend will help diminish conflicts. Would we ask a friend to do some of the household chores that we nag our teens about? Think about how we ask. Would we speak harshly to a friend as we do when frustrated with our teen? Dallas Willard says it well, "Most families would be healthier and happier if their members treated one another with the respect they would give to a perfect stranger."[21]

Change with the Changes

As teens grow and mature, we will have to "get to know him or her" in different ways at different ages. This is true for grandparents as well. We have to keep the relationship going through every phase, because many factors change. We want to respect the person teens are becoming, and show interest in whatever we can. This means spending time with them without an agenda. Just be glad to be together.

You may be asking yourself, "Well, does accepting and listening mean I never speak to anything that I disagree with?" Of course not. We looked at that in the section on good shame messages. What makes the difference is how, when, and how many times we speak to an issue. Do we speak with condemnation? Do we interrupt in anger out of frustration? Do we attack in front of other people? Do we bring issues up over and over? None of these methods will help the relationship. Believe me; our teens and young adults know exactly what we think about most everything. Their brains developed that skill at a very early age. They do not need another lecture; they need love and acceptance. We can love without condoning behavior. What shows on our faces and in our voice tones greatly determines if our teens feel loved.

---

[21] *The Divine Conspiracy*, Dallas Willard, page 219

Failures and Consequences

If our family has walked in grace through the years, failures will be easier to deal with. If not, failures will bring toxic shame and grief when handled with condemnation. Part of letting go is not getting in the way of failures and consequences. All of us learn best from failures if allowed to go through them. It does not help teens to get "bailed out" of a logical consequence.

Here are some examples of logical consequences: Not doing homework brings bad grades, which might mean attendance at summer school or hindrance into a preferred college. Not helping with laundry might leave one without favorite clothes. Not saving money might prevent a desired purchase. As parents, we do better to be supportive and accepting without bailing out. Too many people today feel that they are victims and take little or no responsibility for their problems. Don't try to prevent every failure. Let your young person learn as much as possible *before* he or she leaves home. One of my friends recently texted this question about her sixteen year old:

Friend:
H. has to be at work in 45 minutes. Should I wake him up?

Me:
Don't wake him up unless you have not told him before that you will not wake him up.

Friend:
I have not told him that.

Me:
Then go wake him up but then make it very clear that you will not be doing that anymore. You want him to do this himself. If he doesn't get up and is late he will have a logical consequence.

Friend:
OK. Thanks.

This friend is working very hard to make the changes and transitions necessary to help her teen grow into the Adult Stage. She is working hard and praying often as she learns to let go of control. She texted me the other day to say that H., who had his new driver's license, was driving to Six Flags with a friend. I was proud of her for staying quiet as she watched him drive away on this very scary adventure. Many prayers went up until he returned safely back home.

CHAPTER NINE: WHAT IF I'VE "LOST" THE RELATIONSHIP WITH MY TEEN?

Perhaps like Lisa and John, others of us did not parent well in the younger years because of ignorance, lack of skills, or issues with our unresolved wounds. Now we have a withdrawn, grouchy, and maybe even rebellious teen. In a later chapter I will speak about rebellion, but for now let's look at situations that are less extreme. Over the years I have noticed that conscientious Christian parents have a lot of trouble letting go when the teen years arrive. Homeschooling parents are accustomed to being with and knowing where their children are almost 24/7. Other parents live by too many rules, or the home has a low-joy environment. Relationships are strained, but the teens are still at home and some parents desire to do the hard work to rebuild and reconnect.

We have heard from Lisa how she made intentional efforts to re-connect with Jason. As the weeks went by Lisa began to approach her other son, Jonathan, to try to re-connect with him. It took a little more effort to break through Jonathan's resistance, but Lisa persevered. She invited him to lunch occasionally with *no agenda* to talk about anything. As she had with Jason, Lisa communicated that she was glad to be with Jonathan and backed way off on nagging about chores and his preferences. Here is a story that I love because Lisa is so teachable and humble. We laugh often when she texts with me on ways to respond to her teens differently than she has in the past.

Lisa:
I asked Jonathan if he would like for me to take him to the Bass Pro Shop. He wants to take a friend. What should I do?

Me:
TAKE. THE. FRIEND. Always take the friend with a teen.

Lisa:
But I wanted this to be me and him time.

Me:

That is an agenda. Just be glad to be with him. No agendas!

Lisa:

Lol! (*and lots of emojis*) OK. I get it!

As Lisa and John began filling their house with joy and synchronizing, they had to decide which hills they would pick to "die" on. They let up on some music, movies, and TV shows that had been forbidden, leaving the boys more leeway to choose. Remember how Lisa decided to watch a TV show with Jonathan instead of forbidding it? Here is another way that Lisa and John changed their "rules."

Making Scary Changes

Around the same time that Jonathan was watching the Grimm TV program, he asked me if he could begin using the Instagram social networking app. At that point we had not allowed either of our sons to use social media because of the negative results shown in studies I had heard about. Because I had been so focused on controlling him rather than knowing him, I didn't even realize or care that he was the only teenager he knew who didn't have Instagram or some type of social networking app. (I realize now how that must have made him feel.)

Though it was extremely hard, I decided to let go and trust him. At first I was feeling anxious about the amount of time he spent checking his Instagram and I felt tempted to control his use. I received encouragement from Barbara to let him try his wings while I focused on the relationship. I began sitting down next to him while he was checking Instagram and I would scratch his back. He began sharing posts with me, and we started laughing together! After a recent retreat with his friends, he shared with me the pictures his friends were posting from the retreat and I really got to know him as a result! As it turns out, Instagram is giving us more to talk about and is actually helping our relationship!

I love how teachable and brave Lisa is. She and John have slowly but surely seen their family change tremendously. Both Lisa and John attended my workshops, came for Jesus to heal their past unresolved hurts, and asked their boys to forgive the past mistakes they had made as parents. John saw so much change in Lisa that he asked to join our ladies' Joy Group. Now we have a co-ed group with three men in our community learning how to apply joy and retrain their brains. And I must say again, the most important thing I've seen in Lisa and John is how they are teachable and humble. They are vulnerable and honest about their mistakes in the past as well as when they struggle now. They are open to others' input and then they go away and practice it. Watching God transform an entire family has blessed me beyond words.

Lisa and John are a testimony to God's transformation when we do our part and rely on Him for His. They already had a walk with God, and their family was based on God's ways as best they knew. But I realize some readers could be reading a parenting book when they feel they have done very little to bring their teen up in the Lord and His ways. A teen or young adult may be troubled and difficult to deal with. Maybe someone in the family just became a Christian. Maybe a parent just got their own life straightened out. Maybe the parents did their best *as* a Christian and still a teen is rebellious and/or pushing away. For whatever reason a teen or young adult may be rebellious or estranged, the pain is huge. Is there anything that will help? It is my hope that gaining some understanding of the teen years will comfort the pain and bring some hope.

I know firsthand that living with a rebellious teenager brings conflict, chaos, and pain to everyone involved. I know this pain as a parent—and as a grandparent. It's useless to blame ourselves or to blame each other. At best we just want to avoid hopeless despair and get past the problem. We have to turn to God. He is the best help we can find.

CHAPTER TEN: GOD'S DESIGN FOR ADOLESCENCE

God has a plan for human development and this book is a small part of how to follow that plan. Life Model Works has contributed to our understanding with their Maturity Stages, brain science, and Immanuel healing prayer. Being outside of God's plan is very painful even when the reason is simple ignorance. In order to soften the edges of pain we feel with a rebellious or troubled teen, I would like to approach the problem from two directions by asking a two-part question: Is the teen rebellious or is he or she trying to individuate (try their wings)? Parents often think all teen problems are rebellion. They are not the same.

As I understood the role that individuation plays during the teen years it helped me tremendously as I hit bumps with my own teens, my grandchildren, and with people to whom I minister. Individuation is an aspect of the teen years that I learned about from John and Paula Sandford, founders of Elijah House, a counseling ministry in Idaho, and authors of the book, *Transformation of the Inner Man.*[22]

The Sandfords include individuation in their discussion of three lessons that children should learn during their teen years. These three lessons go right along with the Adult maturity tasks we looked at in Chapter Seven. These lessons are necessary in order for teens to form a group identity, to be able to "leave and cleave" in marriage, and to have healthy relationships throughout life. The three lessons are individuation, incorporation, and internalization. Let's define each of these separately.

Individuation is the process that involves separating oneself from all formative influences and becoming one's own person (p. 330 *Transformation of the Inner Man*). This process can be a difficult task as the teen struggles to become his own person while remaining part of a

---

[22] *Transformation of the Inner Man*, John and Paula Sandford, Victory House Inc., Tulsa, OK, 1982

family. But without individuation, a person cannot incorporate (form a group identity) healthily.

Incorporation means to become part of a group (community, family, marriage) and to have sensitivity to the desires and wishes of others. Individuation is necessary for healthy incorporation, because only a truly free person can give himself to a group and accept the give and take of a healthy relationship. (p. 330 TIM) When we look at the Adult Stage tasks in the *Life Model*,[23] we can see how many of those tasks involve incorporation with others.

Internalization is the other necessary ingredient for healthy incorporation. First the teen must individuate (cut free) and then he must internalize for himself all that he has seen, heard, and learned about life. The values he's been taught must become his own, often by painful inner wrestling. There is no shortcut. (p. 331 TIM)

This entire process takes courage on the part of the teen and patience on the part of parents. Various forms of individuation have been in process since birth—separation from the womb followed by, "I can do it myself," around the age of two. Now in the teen years, individuation will come to fullness. It will take time and patience. It will be necessary to go through this time in joy—being glad to be together.

Partly what makes individuation difficult is that the teen will go back and forth between his desire to stand against his parents and the need to remain in the safety of childhood. He has to stand against the very people he loves and admires. (p. 332 TIM) Parents will notice that one day they demand independence and the next they act like a child. Our reactions play a huge part in how things turn out.

Just because the teen wrestles with our values does not mean that all our training was useless. Very often the fact that the teen has the courage

---

[23] *Life Model, Living from the Heart Jesus Gave You*, or *Living With Men*, www.lifemodelworks.org

to individuate and internalize is proof that we did a good job. Let that be part of what we hold on to during difficult circumstances.

As they separate, examine, and test all values for themselves, sometimes consciously and other times subconsciously, teens may be asking themselves, "Is God real? Do I want to follow Him? What do I believe about Him, about politics, about the world, and about life?" Each teen must wrestle with questions like these and have the freedom to search and make them his or her own. This is not an easy process and has to be "felt" down deep in the spirit. "Incidents have to happen which reveal to the teen, often by pain and loss, where his heart really stands." (p. 333 TIM)

The Worst Response

Timing is as important to this threefold process as it was to the windows best suited for brain development the first two years. God has ordained that individuation, internalization, and incorporation should take place in the teen years. The worst thing that parents can do as the process begins is to clamp down, tighten up rules, lecture, nag, and attack. It is vital to stay supportive and let go as much as possible, allowing plenty of room for unconditional acceptance as he tries to discover what he truly wants and believes. If we clamp down and tighten up, the teen may have to "defend the very things he might have used to discover reality and come to sensibility." Then he may have to go to worse depths in order to break loose. He might get stuck in ways that he would not have taken if everyone had not come down so hard. (p. 335 TIM) "Let them go," say the Sandfords. "This does not mean permissiveness. Guidelines must remain. We speak of an *inner* letting go expressed outwardly as compassion and understanding." (p. 340 TIM)

Inner Letting Go

Let me elaborate for a moment on what I feel that inner and outer letting go may look like, and later I will share some stories to illustrate both. Inner letting go is an attitude that comes from our heart. It means that we allow our teen (or anyone) to follow his or her own journey. It means that we do not reject the person for choices, ideas, directions, or preferences that they have. We might not agree, but we do not reject the person. We interact without strife and put-downs. There is no way that parents can do this without trusting God. And to trust God, we must know what He is like. During the teen years, especially, we must be leaning on the Heavenly Father who is full of grace, mercy, faithfulness, and who has our best interest at heart.

Outward Letting Go

How we speak to and interact with a young person with whom we disagree characterizes outward letting go. Will we nag and belittle, or communicate compassion and understanding? Can we agree to disagree? We may need to allow more freedom of movement in and out of our home. We may have to lighten up on rules. It will be important to keep practicing our joy skills.

It's possible to let go outwardly and not let go inwardly, or vice versa. As our teen grows to adulthood, much of what he or she does will not be "any of our business." Some parents never let go inwardly and that causes many extended family problems such as interference after marriage. Some parents never let go outwardly and a teen may move towards rebelling or leaving home. Parents' willingness to let go is a huge factor in the process of individuation.

Preventing individuation at the proper time in the teen years will brew deep underlying trouble that will likely erupt at a later time—when there are a spouse and children involved. Many family problems arise when a father or mother decides to act like a teenager—partying, carousing, and as the Sandfords say, "opting for the wild life." (p. 339) If a person has to individuate later than the teen years, it will take lots of help, counseling, and repair to get them and others involved through the mess. Wise parents will turn loose at the ordained time.

The Prodigal Son

In the New Testament there is a great example of individuation and how it is best handled. That is the story in Luke 15 of the Prodigal Son. John Sandford gives a clear interpretation of this story. The younger son left home with his inheritance, which was the same as wishing his father were dead. He took hold of what was his in order to individuate and internalize. It cost him everything—a very hard lesson to learn. What happened when the son returned is the place in the story where we want to concentrate. Most of us have had teaching about the father's forgiveness and restoration and how he is like God waiting for our return. That is, of course, very key and important. But let's look at the story from a different angle. What can we learn from the fact that upon his return the father gave his son the ring, a new robe, and a celebration? John Sandford says that the father recognized that the son had become his own man and was now qualified to rule. Not just in spite of his rebellion, but also because of it, the father rejoiced that his boy had come through it all and returned a man (p.333).

Sandford completes the story with strong words. "The remark of the elder brother is easily seen by any experienced counselor as that of an un-individuated child: 'Look! For so many years I have been serving you, and I have never neglected a command of yours and you have never given me a kid, that I might be merry with my friends, but when this son of yours came, who has devoured your wealth with harlots, you killed the fatted calf for him.'" (Luke 15: 29-30) Internalization means that as much as a teen may admire his parents and desire to keep their moral ways, he must not simply do so [blindly and without examination] or he fails to become his own person. He must examine morality for himself, test, and see." (p. 333)

This discussion brings Sandford to another heavy point. "Can Jesus' comparison of the prodigal and elder sons say among other things, that He views maturation in Christ as more valuable than being good? Suppose we have two children, one who stumbled many times and returned through it all to be wise and free, while the other is a model of good behavior, but with whom we can't be fully real because he is always performing to please us. Which son are we more relaxed with? Which one is truly a son? Which is like a servant trying to please us? The one who has become a son is the one with whom we have a depth of fellowship the performer knows nothing about." (Paraphrased, p 340 TIM)

As I began to learn these ideas from the Sandfords, I had to chew on them, pray about them, and examine them. They resonated deep in my heart and brought hope to my pain whenever I encountered an issue that seemed wayward or rebellious in my teens. Both John and Paula, and I, can testify today that these truths work. During the time that their book came out and they were building a worldwide ministry, one of their sons was wayward and rebellious. I listened to his story on cassette and soaked in John's admonition to "keep the relationship no matter the behavior (by not rejecting or condemning the teen) so that when he or she is ready to return, *you* will be standing there as the one they come back to." That son became the head of Elijah House.

And today my "teens" that individuated and internalized have incorporated well with their spouses and community while owning most all the values their father and I desired for them. I thank God for the lessons that John and Paula taught me about wayward teens. Those years were some of the most painful I've lived through, but God's grace and my understanding of individuation kept the pain bearable as I clung to Him. I had to let go. I had to know what God is like and trust Him, believing that He loves my children more than I do.

Letting Go is Painful

Letting go was like tearing out part of my heart. As I let go both inwardly and outwardly, letting go meant saying to two of my teens, "This is your life. You have to live it yourself. You have to pay your consequences. You know what we believe and value. So as you go your way, (late high school on) all we ask is that you don't break any laws or go against any of our values *while on our property*. What you do other places will be your decision, but we expect you to honor us here." Letting go meant that I had to love unconditionally, respect strange decisions, watch silently, and pray. It meant that no matter how much it hurt to watch, I had to leave them in God's hands. The only way to walk with a wayward, individuating teen is on your knees. (I will share their stories in a later section)

Do They Have To Rebel?

As we continue to look at individuation and internalization, let's look at another question. "Can a young person individuate and internalize without rebellion and immorality? The answer to that question is a wonderful, "Yes." The Sandfords are in no way condoning or glorifying sin. But as John says, ". . . if a child cannot individuate any other way, I am sure the Lord would rather he rebel and so become his own person rather than remain a performing Pharisee. I believe our Lord paid the price on the Cross for sons to become sons, not servants only." (p. 340) John and Paula tell their stories in order to give a word of hope and faith to those whose teens are still rebelling.

At the beginning of this section, I proposed that we look at "rebellion" from two directions: Is a teen rebellious or is he or she trying to individuate? I would like to propose that there are differences based on the intensity of the teen's behavior. Rebellion would be the most intense, and in my opinion is most often caused by pain from unresolved wounds. Individuation would be the other end with various degrees of "waywardness" in between. So what are some factors that affect the degree of individuation that makes the child wayward versus turning him to rebellion?

It seems to me that one factor that distinguishes degrees of intensity in individuation would have to do with the level of involvement we have had as parents—how we have disciplined and how we have brought God into the preteen years. According to the Sandfords and other experts, all children need to individuate, internalize, and incorporate. On the lesser end of the intensity scale, some teens who have been reared in the Lord, with parents that walked the talk and filled the home with joy and grace, will only need low levels of "waywardness." This might simply take place in the teen's mental wrestling. It might take the form of disagreeing with parental admonitions, leaning towards a different political party, or bucking against going to church for a season. It might mean finding a different church or a different denomination to attend. It might be choosing music, movies, and TV that have been forbidden. Moving along on the scale of intensity might bring lying, sneaking, arguing, and disrespect, but all in all, the young person seems to be able to remain in the family setting.

Another factor that may keep the intensity mild would be the teen's own walk with God, which could already be strong by this age. Some teens never really rebel against God even though they may question things taught by earthly authorities. Abusing drugs, behaving violently, or running away from home are more extreme.

Rebellion

Rebellion can come from many factors, most of which in my opinion involve unresolved childhood pain. Type **A** and Type **B** traumas affect the growing child and if unhealed can explode into extreme behavior when the child reaches the teens. Children that have suffered neglect, abuse, or apathy from caregivers can be primed for rebellion. The availability of free time, mobility in vehicles, and influential friends are all contributors to the extremes, even when parents did their best. All people have a free will that they can exercise whenever they wish.

But I do lean towards the underlying problem in most rebellion being deep wounds and pain, most likely unrecognized and/or unresolved. If a teen has unresolved traumas, he or she will need help from a counselor and hopefully find a loving community to help growth to resume after the trauma is healed. If drugs, violence, abuse, or running away are impacting the family, let someone know the needs and get help.

Rose's Story

As we looked at briefly in Chapter Five, my granddaughter, Rose, is a good example of a wayward teen whose parents did their best. As we will hear at the end of her story, she acknowledges such as she takes ownership of her rebellious behavior. Along with suicidal thoughts, trying Pot, and an eating disorder, Rose's anger was affecting everyone in her family. She was put on lockdown for over a month. Her parents were considering sending her away to a facility. She had no phone for the whole summer and someone had to be monitoring her most of the time. Punishment was not helping. Everyone was experiencing extreme pain.

No one was asking her "why?" What a painful mess! Let's look at some things that helped us work through this mess after Rose's Dad asked me to check it out.

The first issue I worked on with Rose was her feelings and thoughts about suicide. I asked Rose to tell me the thoughts that were going through her mind when she felt like killing herself. As she told me the thoughts, all beginning with, "I'm_____," I wrote them down. When she finished I went back over each and asked Rose, "Is this true about Jesus?" She answered no to each one. I began to tell her that if these things were not true about Jesus, they were not true about her. She listened. Then I briefly showed her a diagram about Romans 6, Galatians 2:20, II Corinthians 5:17, and Colossians 3: 1-4 to illustrate that whatever happened to Jesus happened to her and whatever was true of Him was true of her. I told her that all the thoughts she had in her mind were not hers. Some, the lies, were from the enemy, and she did not have to listen to them. I gave her a list of ways to distinguish God's voice from Satan's. (See Appendix.) Months later when I asked her what we had done that helped her most, her answer was this discussion.

A bit later we did some spiritual warfare against the enemy and Jesus took her to a memory where she had been frightened in her bed around the age of five. Jesus showed her that a demon had taken hold and was telling her to kill herself. She did not want it and it left. (If you are not familiar with spiritual warfare, please check out the website below for books or articles.)[24] After this session there were only one or two more times that Rose felt suicidal. One of those was when the level of pain at home got extremely high, but she made it through until we could talk.

For a while Rose continued to experience ups and downs. Watching her, and seeing what Mom and Dad were going through, was very painful for me. Wondering what the outcome would be and how long the mess would last caused huge pain as I prayed and cried with Jesus to keep her safe. I had verified that she knew Jesus was in her heart. Over and over I

---

[24] deeperwalkinternational.org

saw how Rose's toughness was a façade to cover her soft heart that was hurting so deeply. She took one step forward, two back.

As I felt my pain with Jesus one evening I heard Him say in my mind, "Focus on the GOOD steps." I wrote this on a card and taped it to my mirror. I clung to Him and His words of comfort and reassurance that He loved Rose and had the situation in His hands. Remembering to focus on the good steps helped me keep the relationship bigger than the problem. Rose did not need condemnation and punishment; she needed unconditional love.

Rose was terrified she was going to be sent away. We talked and prayed. We claimed Proverbs 21:1--"The king's heart is like channels of water in the hand of the LORD; He turns it wherever He wishes"-- asking God to prevent her being sent away. We trusted the Lord would be in control over her "Daddy, the king." That prayer was answered. I was so grateful because I believed sending her away would only make her worse. I was relieved because I knew the answer increased her faith in God.

As I said in Chapter Five, in order to find healing for the unresolved pain that was feeding her acting out, Rose and I did Immanuel Prayer[25] together. Jesus healed the root of her pain. It came from an event where she lost someone very important to her. During another Immanuel session Jesus showed Rose the root of her eating disorder. It began when her fifth grade teacher made fun of her weight in front of the class. Jesus healed that root as well and made it possible for Rose to learn better eating habits and attitudes about food.

When school ended I was able to get Rose three to four days a week. I took her with me to swim lessons I taught. We went to lunch. We went to the thrift store or to Target. (Lunch and the thrift store or Target continued as a weekly outing for almost two years. We still get together at least once a month.) There are times that I wonder if the time spent doing things just for fun and being together had as big an impact on Rose's

---

[25] See the *Share Immanuel* booklet by Wilder and Coursey, www.lifemodelworks.org I will add a brief description to the Appendix.

recovery as anything else. All the time I spent with Rose during those months was totally agenda free. I was not about trying to "fix" her. I did very little correcting. No nagging. If we did "counseling" it was grace-filled, glad-to-be-together time, and non-condemning. If I had no proof of bad behavior, I said nothing, even if I had suspicions.

Once I blew it by asking Rose a question that implied accusation. Rose got up and stomped to the other side of the room. I sat quietly and waited for her to come back. I asked her forgiveness for what I'd said, and told her I wasn't going anywhere until we were OK. In a bit she let me hug her and then I felt her arms go around my waist. We returned to joy.

One day I asked Rose to draw a fork in the road. (She's artistic and I'm not.) As she looked at the fork, I asked her, "If you stay on this road you are on, what will your life be like in five years?" As she thought a minute I asked, "How old will you be in five years?" I could see the wheels turning. Then we considered where her life would be in ten years if she stayed on that fork. Rose exclaimed with no prompting from me, "Nana! No one has ever shown me the big picture of life!" If we go back to Chapter Seven and look at the Child Maturity Stage, we will see that learning the big picture of life is one of the needs. I had never said that phrase to Rose.

As we were driving one day, Rose and I talked about what satisfies. She quickly agreed that being in trouble was not satisfying. We decided that a good meal, having fun together, and having someone with us who loves us unconditionally were all very satisfying. Many times after that as we were driving home, I would ask Rose, "So, what was satisfying today?" She would tell me her list. Knowing what satisfies is a Child Stage task.

Through the summer Rose and I worked on various relational and maturity skills. She learned how to notice her Relational Circuits were off and get them back on (Chapter Two). We talked about forgiveness. Dr. Wilder says that it can be difficult for teens to forgive because they don't want to add up how big the offense actually is and so they realize at some level that if they forgive it will not be for the whole problem.[26] I helped Rose see that she could forgive parts of what had hurt her and that forgiving has nothing to do with what the offender has done, but rather all to do with us who are doing the forgiving. We are not condoning their behavior or saying it doesn't matter; we admit and work through our hurt, then choose to forgive.[27] Eventually she was able to forgive.

It was important for Rose to learn how to suffer well and stay relational during difficulties. Part of that was what we looked at in Chapter Five—seeing positive characteristics of her heart. One day I told her some of my own pain and struggles. Knowing how old I am, her response was, "Are you saying having pain never goes away?" I answered, "Yes! And that is why we have to learn to suffer well." (See Chapter Five)

Through the summer emotions settled down at home as Rose began to stabilize. Mom, Dad, and I began to talk more, although I did not tell them details about my times with Rose. Since there was little contact with friends, Rose had less and less trouble. Right before school started Daddy gave her phone back. But the struggles and lessons were not over.

Shortly after school began, association with the questionable friends resumed. As Mom, Dad, and I talked, we decided to let go and let Rose truly individuate, make her decisions, and come to the end of whatever it was she needed to learn. They would only confront her if they had undeniable proof that she was acting out. She was freer to come and go.

As time went by, we intentionally refrained from focusing on any suspicions we had. We left her in God's hands and prayed. Over that year God orchestrated a few incidents involving the police and her questionable friends that showed Rose where she really wanted to land. We could see the changes and growth.

---

[26] Taken from my book *Re-Framing Your Hurts*, page 44, barbaramoonbooks.com or amazon.com

[27] For more details on healthily seeking forgiveness, granting forgiveness, and receiving forgiveness, see Chapter 6 in my book, *Living Lessons on Intimacy with Christ*, 2013, barbaramoonbooks.com or amazon.com

Rose and I were still meeting for fun and shopping and I often heard her talk about what she had learned and how different she felt. One day she said, "Nana! Just look at me! A year ago I was a mess and wanting to kill myself. I am so glad I'm alive!" I do believe the loving bond we shared was part of her recovery. I was as blessed and learned almost as much as Rose did. She called me her best friend and gave me a special nickname. Every time she texted me the nickname I got tears in my eyes. I was so grateful that she was alive, well, and growing.

After Rose turned from the questionable friends, she began to act more consistently like the person we knew her to be. Within the next year, she became more interested in spiritual things and asked to be baptized. At her church, candidates may choose who baptizes them. Rose chose her sister, Marie. As I listened to Rose vulnerably read her testimony, heard her confess how messed up her life had been, and talk about how she came back to Christ, I could barely hold back my tears. When I watched her sister baptize her, I wept. When I hugged her soaking wet neck, I could no longer hold it back and I burst into sobs. There were no words for my gratitude to Jesus for all He had done in Rose's life.

Healing and Redemption

God is all about salvation, healing, restoration, and redemption. Rose's story has a joyful ending and most of that is because we turned to Him and His people for help. And Rose did her part. Before the healing and redemption of a teen's story though, it's very painful to face that he or she is not doing well. It's even more painful to have no clue as to the outcome. We don't even want to admit that our teen might have some kind of pain that's causing their behavior. We feel like a failure and fear facing our part in the problem. Regardless of what caused the mess—our failures, our ignorance, or the teen's choices—pain and regret are huge. There is no way out of this mess if God doesn't do something; we need Him in order to make it through. We will have to trust Him and come to see from His perspective.

As we walk through all that's involved when a teen or young adult is acting out, it will help if we can come to a place to face our part in our teen's pain. Everyone needs restoration and forgiveness and that won't happen if everyone doesn't get help and work through all the factors. It doesn't really matter if we failed out of ignorance or particular mistakes; the teen needs to hear us humbly own up and ask forgiveness for our lacks. They, of course, have to do the same for their part.

Estranged Relationships

In some families, an older teen or young adult might be estranged, not speaking to parents or joining family functions. In those cases, we can pray and do our best to reconnect with joy-filled skills when we do have contact. Sometimes taking an estranged son or daughter out to lunch will help—*IF* we have no agenda other than being glad to be with them. They will sense the difference and respond better to unconditional love that doesn't nag or correct. It's better not to bring up controversial issues or talk about why they don't want to be with us. It might be a slow process to rebuild, but using our relational joy skills makes restoration possible.

Because having wayward or estranged young people in our lives is so painful, some of us will tend to take *all* the blame. We will need to remind ourselves that *all* is not our fault. Young people have a will and mind of their own. Keep in mind that whatever is going on with a wayward teen, everyone needs grace to believe that the teen is just "working on his or her testimony," and that "the Lord will heal the land that the locusts have eaten." (Joel 2:25) Pray, trust the Lord, and leave no room for condemnation. Be glad to be with them any time possible.

CHAPTER ELEVEN: HOW DO THE RULES CHANGE?

The basic rules we've had "posted" for years—be kind and respect others—will never change, but during the teen years, we may interpret and enforce them a bit differently. The rules will become more like guidelines. We will no longer be able to use physical force to pick that kid up and move him to another activity. They will be impossible to control. The consequences for acting unkindly or disrespectfully will be different. We don't have to turn small things into major skirmishes. But there will be times to speak to issues with our Relational Circuits on. There will be many opportunities for logical consequences. Remember when my friend's son was about to be late for work if he didn't get up?

Guidelines and Boundaries

Teens may act out for various reasons, but guidelines and boundaries are part of life. It will be good to distinguish between guidelines and boundaries. As long as the teen is "under our roof" there will be a place for both. Guidelines are something we give in hopes they will follow them with logical consequences if they don't; boundaries are something *we* decide that *we* will keep for ourselves and what we will do if the teen decides to be a guideline or boundary buster. We cannot control another person's behavior (guidelines) but we can control what our limit (boundary) will be concerning another's behavior.

Guidelines about respect might include letting someone know when we are leaving and about when we will return. Expecting decent communication and voice tone would be a guideline. A boundary would be saying something like, "If you are going to talk to me like that, I am going to leave until we can talk calmly." The boundary is about us, not them. Teens sometimes sound disrespectful because they are hurting and don't feel heard, understood, or loved. They are "yelling" for understanding and help. As Lisa did when she realized Jason's behavior was because he was triggered, stop and notice; listen. And when there is a guideline or boundary given and parents hear, "Whatever!" or "Argggghhhh!" it's best to just ignore these responses—especially if just

© 2017 Barbara Moon

done once during that encounter. Young people are "saving face." We need to let that go and zip our lips.

No Hypocrisy

As we saw in Chapter Eight we want to move towards treating our teens and young adults as we would another adult. Teens want some kind of fair and understandable guidelines in order to feel secure and know what to expect. All guidelines and boundaries should be very clear and consistently followed by appropriate and predetermined consequences. The guidelines should be held to a *grace-filled minimum.* Parents need to keep guidelines and boundaries as well. Teens are very astute at noticing hypocrisy. They do not like to be told not to do something they see the parent doing. They do not like to be told to do something the parent is not doing. Shawnda has some wisdom about helping lessen contention in our family relationships.

Preferences

I was pondering for a few days with the Lord about relationships. My main question was about relationships and what is it that causes contention between people. I don't believe that there is just one thing, but I did ask Jesus if He would show me something about it. Over the course of a few days I questioned others when I heard about their troubles with other people. Minor troubles of disagreements and such were what seemed to be standing out.

One evening my husband and I were doing dishes together and loading the dishwasher and he let me know that from now on we should run the dishwasher at night and unload it every morning. This was stated matter-of-factly, not exactly usual from him, and I had questions! "Why? What's with the new rule?" He nonchalantly said "Oh, it's just a preference."

AHA! Preferences. That was a key to my ponderings! Did you ever realize that you have made a rule out of a preference? I have for sure. I have decided that I like something a certain way, and told the whole house full of people that "from now on, it will be this way," and suddenly I saw attitudes and issues galore. With this new insight the Lord showed me that when I did that I had just issued a law. And by the way, when I had done this kind of rule in the past I had not practiced mutual satisfaction. I had not inquired about anyone else's preferences before making my new rule!

How will my kids or those around me ever learn their personal preferences if they don't have the option to explore them? I believe that asking about someone's preferences makes them feel important? This can be practiced with our teenagers from the beginning of their adult stage at age 12-13, and most certainly with every relationship we have.

Part of our teens becoming their own person is reflected in the Child Tasks and the Adult Tasks. The child is to learn self-expression; the adult is to develop a personal style that reflects his or her heart. (See Stages in Chapter Seven and a tip on personal style in Chapter Thirteen.) Knowing what we like and don't like and being free to explore and voice our preferences is part of that process. We might not always get our way, but it's important to have freedom to communicate back and forth within our relationships.

No Bailing Out

As our teen approaches the end of high school, if he or she is somewhat mature and responsible, the guidelines can become increasingly more minimal. When a student goes off to college or the military, he or she can do *anything* they want and we will not know about it. So begin to turn loose that last year they are home. Continue to put more and more responsibility upon their shoulders and allow them to pay the logical consequences of their choices. It does them no good for us to bail them out of consequences just because it hurts us to watch.

We remember Shawnda's stories about Trey's monster truck. She jokingly ended her tale with these words: "It took two years and about a million dollars later before he decided he should sell it. I was thankful to say the least!" Shawnda and her husband watched as that "million dollars" went into the truck and down the drain. Trey spent his own money without complaint as he kept trying to piece it together. Shawnda and Mark never said, "We told you so." They never berated or belittled Trey for his choices. They lovingly supported him and waited on him to decide when it was time to let it go. Trey paid some big, expensive, logical consequences that helped him learn some good lessons about major purchases and money. Helping our teens and young adults understand how money works is a gift towards their future—even if they have to learn it the hard way.

CHAPTER TWELVE: MONEY

Hopefully, our young person has already learned some lessons about money. They have probably earned money by babysitting, mowing grass, or even from having a "real" job. If we instilled the three divisions of money (giving 10%, saving10%, and spending 80%) in our teens when younger, they may or may not stick to this division. Some teens save all they make and others spend all they make. As older teens and young adults, it should be totally up to the teen what he or she does with their money. Do they need to save for college? Do they need to save for a car? Do they need to learn what it's like to run out of money? Let them make their mistakes while still at home—especially if they are working. If they run out of money because they spent it all, we don't give them spending money. That is a logical consequence.

Through the years, I have been amazed at the number of adults who do not know how to handle a checkbook. It's a good life skill to teach our teens before they leave home. They should know how to balance the checkbook each month and why it's important. Perhaps in the future, checking will all be done electronically, but at least make certain that the teen knows how banking works.

Here is another caution: Some laws have been changed about credit card companies hooking young college students with cards. They used to flood the colleges and give kids a card. Now there is an age limit. If we have modeled not living by credit, our student may not fall into the trap. But it is good to have a talk about credit cards before the temptation comes. Retail stores also love to give credit cards to young people. They don't even have to have a job first. They want to hook them early on buying by credit so the card company can have their interest for the rest of life.

What If a Young Adult Wants to Move Out?

While we are looking at money issues, I want to give a guideline for helping the young adults when they are ready to move out and they will have to pay for their expenses. Some will be in college in a dorm or staying at home, but there comes a day when they want to move out to an apartment. We can help them look at what is involved before they get in over their heads.

1. Have the young person research the area in which they want to live. Find the cheapest apartment or house and have them ride by the location to see if they would feel safe living there. Find out how much the deposit is, how much the rent is, and how long the lease has to be for whichever place they decide.

2. Sit down with paper and pen and help the young person list out the above costs. Then add in the approximate monthly fee for electricity, water, gas, cable TV, and internet. How much does each of these need as a deposit up front? If parents don't know, have the young person call to find out.

3. Decide if parent or student is going to pay for car expenses, gas, insurance, and phone. Add in.

4. How many others will they be sharing the place with? Divide the total by that.

5. Look at the amount of money the student is bringing in. Discuss how much if any that parents will help.

This is very important to do for our teens. It's much more expensive these days to move out. If a student graduates from college and wants to live at home, it's important that they keep a job and perhaps pay a little rent. When ours were getting started, we took their small amount of rent and put it aside. When the young person moved out or got married, we gave them the money back. One of my sons has done the same thing. The idea here is to help the teens/young adults understand how the real world works. Remember—we are raising adults.

CHAPTER THIRTEEN: DRIVING, DATING, AND CURFEWS

When a young person begins to date and go out with friends in cars, our relationship with the Lord will take a big leap. We will learn to let go of even more things we cannot control. Try to rely on Jesus instead of worrying up into the night. The enemy loves to give us what I heard a teacher long ago call "vain imaginations." This Bible teacher took the words from Romans 1:21 (KJV) and described vain imaginations as allowing one's thoughts to race out of control, imagining the worst. I really understood this teacher's interpretation of vain imaginations the first time I watched my oldest son, Jim, who had just gotten his license, drive out of the driveway, his little sister, Jodi, in the front seat. Before they got to the stop sign, I had their funeral planned. Those kinds of thoughts are vain imaginations and will take us to unnecessary worry.

In some states now, a new driver cannot take non-siblings or others under eighteen in a car with them until they have been driving for six months. Talk to your teen about the seriousness of driving a car and having others' lives in their hands. Talk about dangers of using their phones while driving. Assess your teen's maturity and sensibility before allowing a license. It does not have to be automatic. Let it be known early on that having the license is a privilege. And please be sure to practice the whole year with the Learner's Permit.

Dating

I don't have lots of set tips and rules for dating. Whatever the family's decision about age and activities might be, it is good to let these guidelines be known way before they are needed, maybe in middle school. I would encourage you to extend the age as long as possible and encourage lots of group activities as long as possible. We required young men who wanted to take our daughter out to ask her dad the first time. Our boys asked their girls' fathers for permission to take the girls to the prom or homecoming. One of my sons has kept this tradition with his girls. It can be very helpful to have boys (girls) that want to go out with a daughter (son) spend time with the family in order for parents to get to know them. Having the other young people hang out at your house gives a little control in a very uncontrollable season of a teen's life. The key to having the others at your house is to be a family who is open, joyful, fun, grace-filled, and accepting. And you might need to be sure you have some snacks.

If our teens struggle with peer pressure during this season of life, give them the option of making their parents the "bad guy." They can tell friends that their parents don't allow any activity that they really don't want to participate in. That will make it easier to say, "No."

Curfews

My views on curfews were a bit different than most parents that I knew when my teens were growing up. It seemed that curfew was an issue that caused much conflict. Parents obsessed over minutes and punishments. Students argued and obsessed over being late.

In our family, the emphasis was not on getting home at an exact minute. The time was general and the kids had a say so according to the event. I do not remember one single hassle over curfew from the high school years of our four teens. They did not abuse the trust. It was part of letting go. Our emphasis was on courtesy to always tell us that they were leaving, tell us where they were going, and about what time they would return. Let this be a time of treating them as we would another adult in the household.

CHAPTER FOURTEEN: MISCELLANEOUS TIPS

Personal Style and Preference

As much as possible, let's allow our teens to express themselves while guiding them towards that personal style that reflects their heart. Developing that personal style is one of the Adult Stage tasks. As we saw earlier in Shawnda's story about preferences, it's important for teens to have freedom to explore and find out who they are, what they want, and where they are going. They need a sense of purpose that fits their heart. But they must know their heart in order to know how it fits. They must know and see themselves the way God sees them, and move towards following Him, if not already. Knowing who they are builds a solid, steady foundation to meet the challenges that will come as they grow up and leave. If possible help your teen go through the Heart Characteristics exercise in Chapter Five that I did with Rose. Watch for opportunities to point out their heart characteristics as a matter of daily life.

Shaved Heads, Piercings, and Tattoos

One of my granddaughters shaved her head around the age of fifteen. She said God told her to do so because one of her friends was losing her hair from cancer. She grew the hair back and shaved it again-and again. It was interesting to know this teen so well and watch the looks she got from people who did not know her. She had her style for a season and walked it very well, not caring what her peers thought. Styles are always going to change and it's best to keep our comments to ourselves about things that make the problem more important than the relationship.

All kinds of strange hairdos, piercings, and later tattoos can upset parents. These are things that I feel we should leave up to them. I didn't feel that way in years past, but these days it does not seem to be a battle to fight. When they have to change these things to get a job, it will be their choice. Some will think ahead about that. For me, the relationship is more important than a battle over hair, piercings, or tattoos. Grandparents have to be careful how they interact with the younger generation as well. Teens want to be loved and accepted for who they are, not teased or mocked.

Free to Say, "No."

Part of helping our teens find out who they are and what they want is to leave them plenty of room to explore, to disagree with us, and to fail without rejection and condemnation. We have to allow them to tell us, "No." This is part of treating the teen/young adult as an adult. Shawnda has a story about the first time she had the courage to tell Trey he could say no.

Lawn Story

My husband travels for business. One of Trey's chores has been to mow our lawn during my husband's absence. One day the lawn needed mowing and I went to Trey and asked him to mow for his Dad. Right about when the question came out of my mouth, in my mind, I heard Barbara's voice! Her voice said, "Tell him it's ok to say no." Now that was a crazy thought! For years I had demanded that my kids never say no to us. At this moment though, I had the opportunity to parent in a relational way, instead of a demanding way. So, I said to him that very thing: "It's ok to say no." And he raised his eyebrows at me—and said, "No." In my mind I said to myself, "Alrighty then," as I walked a few steps away. My next thought was a prayer to Heaven. "What do I do now, Lord? This is crazy! If we give him this ok-to-say-no power, surely he will never do another thing I say! Lord, what do I do?"

I heard the Lord say, "Go back in there and ask him about it." I went back in Trey's room and told him I was curious as to why he would say no. He told me because he wasn't motivated to do anything for his Dad right now because Dad wasn't pleased with any of his work. I responded with, "OK. I get that. I see that you are feeling that way and finding it hard to do the mowing right now. Thank you for letting me know." And I walked away.

I had no other thoughts except that it looked like I was the one who would do the mowing! Not long after this exchange, Trey came into the kitchen. He said he was going to wash his Dad's car and he would mow the next day.

"Whoa!" I said to myself. "What just happened?" This is what I believe happened. I believe he felt validated by my response and that I heard him. I believe he felt a new freedom had just been given to him—it's ok to say no. He valued being free to do so. The good news here is, he respects this freedom and does not use it inappropriately. Praise the Lord!

What a great example of having the courage to treat a teen or young adult as we would another adult.

Parents are Parents

We want to be careful not to embarrass our teen when around their friends and classmates. We are not the pal; we are the parent. Teens appreciate it more if a parent acts like an adult and stays sensitive to his or her feelings than that the parent is "cool." Most teens want us to attend their recitals, concerts, and sports events. It's imperative that we schedule our time so that we can attend these functions and behave in a manner that makes them proud. Sometimes that means we are invisible.

Repairing Rivalry

If our early parenting style has caused sibling rivalry, it's possible to repair it. First we need to look honestly at how we have treated the teens when younger and how and if we have compared them to sibs or other people. Comparing and/or favoritism are what cause rivalry

When the time is right, it can be helpful to sit down and confess our part and ask forgiveness. From that time forward, we will need to intentionally spend time with each—time that has no agenda—I'm-glad-to-be-with-you-time. As much as possible, communicate unconditional love and acceptance for what the teen is like. Lisa has a story about how she asked her teens forgiveness for comparing them and showing favoritism.

Sibling Rivalry

Sibling rivalry has been decaying the relationship between my now teenage sons over the past 10 years. It intensified over the past 4 years to a point of serious difficulty in our family. I read so many books, took my kids to counselors and had tried everything I could think of to resolve this, including trying to accept it as "normal" as I had been told by so many.

In my Joy-Filled Relationships group, I began realizing that the cause of the intense rivalry between my sons was simply the lack of joy in our family and my immaturity as a parent. I had wounds that had never been healed and that prevented me from giving both my sons the full amount of bonding, love, and attention they needed. As a result of my irrational fears, I had been treating my oldest son with favoritism and this had created intense resentment from my youngest son, which turned into constant competition and attempts to "one-up" his brother.

I reached out to Barbara for advice and she suggested I first talk with my oldest son and explain how I had made the mistake of favoring him over his brother out of fear that he was not going to be okay. I told him I was going to change that behavior and welcomed him to let me know how I can help him in the transition. Then, I spoke with my husband and explained the same. Barbara suggested we call a family meeting to start creating a sense of community. We did and I explained again, with my youngest son present, how I had made the mistake of treating the older son with favoritism and that was wrong. I kept the time brief as I told them I was going to change that behavior.

Lisa shows us here how any time we can admit our mistakes and ask our teens' forgiveness, relationships will improve. It's never too late to right wrongs and begin with a clean slate.

Making Friends: Creating Belonging

What if we have a teen who is an introvert and another who is an extrovert? The extrovert has lots of friends and a full social calendar. Maybe the introvert struggles to make friends because he or she is quiet; so he or she thinks it's not OK to be an introvert. It's important to encourage both to see that God made them as they are for a purpose, but the introvert might need some extra encouragement. Being an introvert is not good or bad. It's how God wired them.

Making friends can be hard for any teen. If possible, we can help teens learn that it's up to them to create a sense of belonging around themselves. Many of us wait for others to make us feel like we belong. Creating belonging is about being hospitable and welcoming.

Hospitality shows on our faces in the form of smiles. Hospitality works when we are interested in others. It helps to ask others questions and to be glad to hear their answers. It helps create belonging if we make sure we are not judgmental. Let's encourage our introvert teens to have the courage to step out of a comfort zone and see if *they* can create that sense of belonging that seems to come so easy to an extrovert.[28]

Pick Your Battles

Hair, hobbies, sports, music, and clothes are not hills to die on. We want to look at our teen's world through their eyes. How do they feel about things? What is important to them? How can we compromise on questions and decisions that arise? Should a young person take time off from school to work and mature? Can we notice how much we are nagging and correcting instead of treating as we would another adult? Are we talking too much? Should we even consider taking grounding off the table? These are all great questions to consider and discuss. Many problems with teens can be solved by letting go of our expectations, our goals for them, and our bent towards nagging and correcting. I tell the

---

[28] Learned from Dr. Wilder.

moms in my groups all the time, "Zip your lip." "Listen." "Let go." "No agenda."

Shawnda came up with an idea that helps avoid nagging if Trey needs a reminder about something. She sends it to his phone. One time. (Telling someone something more than once is nagging.)

Drugs, Alcohol, and Parties

I don't know what to say about these common vices other than that avoiding them is something that any teen has to do from within. Hopefully what we have taught and modeled will strengthen our teen to say, "No." Being in a good, non-legalistic youth group at a church can help a teen's battle against these temptations. But other than forbidding parties (that we know about) these choices will ultimately be up to the young person. Though it feels like we have some control when they are young, we really never have true control of another person. The teen and young adult years will prove this lack of control to us over and over. The best we can do is cling to God and leave the young people in His hands. We are powerless to control them and we must learn to trust Him and believe that He has their best interest at heart and loves them more than we do. And, where there are difficult issues to bear, that God will bring them through to a better place. No matter what happens, He will be with us. Sometimes, just as Jesus did with His disciples, we have to trust the untrustworthy.

Sex Education

I know sex education begins very young these days whether it is formal or in the locker room. The following is from a teaching given by Pastor Kevin Meyers (PK) who is the senior pastor of 12Stone Church in Gwinnett County, GA. PK, as he is lovingly called, not only models humility and transparency, he models what it means to mentor one's children. I want to paraphrase his message about how he explained dating and pre-engagement relationships to his daughter, Julisa (then a teen). It fits well under this topic. My version will be brief, but I hope that it will at least strike some thoughts for us to ponder.

As Kevin was talking with his daughter one day, she asked about dating. PK drew a diagram to help explain how relationships could be broken down into five categories and what they would mean as she began to "date" and eventually find a mate. The five categories were: acquaintances, friend, boyfriend/girlfriend, engagement, and marriage.

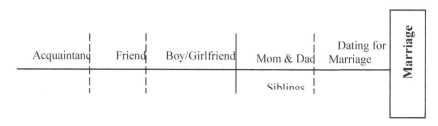

"As you look at having a 'boyfriend'" Daddy told his daughter, "remember that at this point you do not give your heart away. I own your heart. Daddy owns your heart (as does your Heavenly Father). At this point you only give affection, not your heart. As you honor your father and your mother, we will be looking out for your best interest. When you get ready for dating, Mom and I and your siblings will be evaluating boys who cross over our "solid line." If we don't like what we see, he will be sent back to the friend category. As you begin dating for engagement, the family will still be checking things out, and as you will then begin to give your heart away, I'll agree to it if I see God is in it."

Dad went on to say with great passion, "As you begin to give your heart away, you never give your body away. You do not give your body until he has given you his heart and hand in marriage. That is the only condition for giving your body." PK then talked about how nothing works unless God has all of one's heart. Then he finished the diagram talking about how the "marriage box" represents that she will leave her parents and cling to her husband.

This message is available at www.12Stone.com. The date of the teaching was January 15, 2006.

College, Military, or Job

If our teen is college bound, likely he or she has been traveling that direction for a while. Hopefully we have helped them understand the importance of grades through the high school years. We have encouraged them to move towards self-discipline about homework and the balance of outside activities. We want to communicate along the way that they have part of the responsibility of doing well in college, especially if we are paying. If they don't work hard, they can help pay. Knowing they might have to help pay will encourage them to do better. All four of my children found ways to get through college with very little to no help from us and they all graduated with either none or very little debt. At this writing, four grandchildren have graduated with no debt. All valued what they worked hard for and had tangible stories about God's faithfulness.

College may not be on the horizon for our student. They may want to go into the military. Listen to his or her ideas and desires. The principle thing to move towards at this age is "independence" from us and "dependence" upon God. We don't want to be guilty of enabling our young person to lie around playing video games and not move towards that independence. When they graduate high school or reach eighteen, they should be taking care of themselves or contributing to the household if not in college or the military.

Free to Come and Go

By the time a young person goes away to college or the military (or has a full time job) the principle rules when at home should be those that pertain to any adult living in the household. I personally think that within reason a college student should have complete freedom to come and go, but with that freedom they would have a respectful attitude towards others' needs and share responsibilities pertaining to the household when there on weekends or summers. By this time, if we have moved towards treating them like adults, there should be few problems.

If we see grades dropping in high school or college, first determine if there is some problem going on with the teen. Remember our earlier chapters on relational skills such as checking on the Joy Bucket to see if it's full or empty? Find out if the student has experienced an upsetting incident. Use the kind tone and questions we looked at earlier: "It seems you aren't acting like yourself. What's going on? Is there anything I can do to help?" No lectures. No pushing. If the teen is simply goofing off, let him pay his own consequences. If they start to flunk out of college and it's not something we can help with, we might have to let it happen. But he or she can't then "veg" on the couch while we foot the bill.

I Changed My Mind

Should a student go to college for a while and then decide that's not what he wants to do, consider this. I know a young man who was a straight A student in high school who went to college for a year and then wanted to stop and work for a while. His wise parents allowed him to make that decision. He worked for about a year and then returned to college and finished his degree.

One of my grandsons wanted to pursue time in a ministry after his first year of college. His parents supported him as he took some time off to check that out. He eventually returned to work and school.

Another young lady I know went to college for a while and did not do well. She grew very discouraged and wanted to quit and become a cosmetician. Her parents were disappointed, but after some counsel decided to let her go to cosmetology school. She finished her courses there and worked for a while before returning to college and completing her degree.

These are examples of supporting and encouraging our young person as they branch out to find their unique way in life. The years immediately after high school are a very short period of time in relation to the rest of life. There is plenty of time to get a degree if a person wants one.

Tough Love

Sometimes love is tough, especially during waywardness or rebellion. Tough love allows logical consequences. Tough love draws a line, or a boundary, that says, "My *love* for you will not change, but what I *do*, (or allow to go on in our home) for you can change." This kind of love stands back and watches (and grieves) while strong, logical consequences occur. It does not enable or bail out the teen nor keep them from learning a lesson. Sometimes logical consequences can be severe and painful to watch.

Tough lovers hold on to God while they watch, pray, and hurt. They trust that God is bigger than the circumstance. They believe that somewhere in the mess will blossom a testimony for His glory. Tough loving parents walk in the fact that God is in control while they refuse to look at appearances. I know this because I had to walk it myself. With permission, I will share three stories—two stories about tough love, one involving an incident where my third son, Greg, paid some life-changing logical consequences, the other a story from my daughter Jodi's teen years. The third story will illustrate unconditional love and God's faithfulness in spite of appearances.

Greg's Story

In my early teens, I began my "criminal" career. While it was confined to occasional shoplifting during those first years, by the time I turned 16, I was on my way to becoming a full-blown crook (or so I thought). This proclivity towards unlawful behavior could not be attributed to my parents, siblings, or upbringing. It was not because I was a "poor" kid, a "dumb" kid, or a "bad" kid either. Rather it was something that developed within me independent of all external sources.

My parents taught me right from wrong, ensured my attendance at church whenever the doors opened, and provided a moral compass for me to follow with their behavior. I was a nearly straight-A student with plenty to eat, fairly decent clothes, and a roof over my head. Yet none of this was enough to deter me. I simply had a talent and a desire for stealing, and enjoyed the rush of getting away with it.

Looking back, I really have no good reason for taking things that didn't belong to me. My best excuse was that, because of growing up without a lot of extras (needs were provided), I felt I was owed a better life, so to speak. When I saw something I wanted, but couldn't have due to my parents' very practical budget limitations, I did not accept that as my lot in life. Several years of practice led me to my biggest caper in the summer of 1987 prior to my sophomore year of college.

While working at a national grocery chain, I easily discovered a "foolproof" method for stealing money directly from the till. By logging on as an employee that had already left for the day (whose till had thus already been counted down), I was able to perform an undetected transaction and pocket the cash. After nearly three months of milking my employer, I got lazy and was caught, arrested and taken to jail.

Parents, I must tell you that your suspicions that jail is not a safe place are well founded. However, imprisonment (for a very short time comparative to others) was the only possible outcome that could hope to teach me the skills I had somehow grown up ignoring. If your teen is heading down this path, it may be the only way for him to understand that the consequences of his actions will catch up with him. As I sat in stir, I recall with absolute clarity when I finally understood that my behavior would lead to my eventual downfall if I did not mend my ways. The holding tank was also the place that the "real" felons would come to make phone calls, and one particular prisoner marked me for life.

The enormous man sat down directly beside me and began a series of phone calls. As he talked to first his mother, then his girlfriend, and finally his lawyer, I supposed that this gentleman was moving toward redemption. However, when his lawyer began to contradict his assertions of innocence, the convict simply replied (in a loud, booming voice), that he was certain he had not killed the man in question and that his lawyer better get that through his head lest he (the prisoner) feel obligated to "kill him too."

Now, people – you just can't give your child this kind of self-evaluating perspective in a loving Christian home! I decided then and there not to continue my illicit behaviors lest I end up bunkies with a gorilla like the one screaming at his lawyer in the chair next to mine. No matter of nagging, cajoling, threatening, or persuasion by my parents, teachers, or clergy could have ever made such a profound impact as this prisoner did. You simply lack, as a "good" parent, a believable framework for your criminally minded teen to relate to. Sometimes only another criminal can provide the lesson your child needs. It was the case with me, and I can happily say with honesty that I have never been tempted to steal since that day.

While your story may differ, remember that your teen decided very early on whether you would have input into his character. Be consistent, and prepare for the eventuality of county-sponsored discipline (if need be). You can beg, shout, and wave your hands all you want, but it may be something that has to happen in order for your child to become an adult.

Jodi's Story

Well, that story warms a mother's heart, doesn't it? It's not so hard to read now that many years have passed and her son is grown and quite stable. I'm proud to say my sons have all turned out well and along with my son-in-law are great men, husbands, fathers, and leaders. Rearing three sons was fun, but I really wanted a girl.

After trying to adopt in order to have a girl, I got pregnant. I bowed to God's will that it was up to Him now, and a few months later we had our girl and she was (and is) all that I ever dreamed for. We brought her up in the ways of the Lord, and she was courageous enough to individuate and internalize during her junior year of high school. During this time, I learned more than I have time to write here. I had to walk what I'd talked many times and cling to God for about a year as Jodi tried and tested and grew. Not all of it was just individuation, because our unrecognized marriage problems were causing her pain as well. But as issues escalated concerning a boy we did not want her to be with, a day came when we had to ask her to leave our house. We had arranged for her to be with close friends for a month.

With that friend's guidance and help we worked through a plan. Jodi would live with them as an adult, paying "rent" and letting them know how she would be coming and going, mostly being her own boss. With those privileges would come the same responsibilities that an adult carries such as car upkeep, gas, school activity schedules, etc. She already had a good relationship with Scott and Laurel and they encountered no problems during that time. Dad and I did not handle everything well, but with continual sessions with Scott we adjusted our mistakes and stayed in the "tough love" mode. (I was surprised how often I forgot to be tough.)

Towards the end of the month, Jodi asked if she could come back home. When we met with Scott to discuss a new plan, we decided that we would give her the choice to come back as an "adult" with all the privileges, but with the financial responsibilities involved there, or as our "child" and all that involved. She tearfully told us that she wanted to be our "child," that she had broken up with the boy. She returned to finish her teen years with very few hassles and lots of delight for us. God continued to work on her testimony through college and teach her many things as she continued to grow. I would not change anything about my lovely daughter today. She is a true blessing, a good friend, a wonderful wife, and a great Mommy. And she truly loves, obeys, serves, and shares God. What a blessing!

A Young Adult Story

From 2000 to 2010 I lived with my third son, Greg, his wife, Chris, and their family. This time was one of my dearest blessings. Before they married, while Greg was away at college, Chris lived at our house for about a year while she was in college. Chris had been part of my life since she was in the eighth grade and of course I've known Greg all of his life. Knowing both of their stories from their early years just adds to the blessing of being such a part of their lives. After Greg graduated and Chris was still in school, the two of them went through a very difficult lesson. I have their permission to share it.

When Chris came into our lives, she was in the eighth grade and a strong follower of Jesus Christ. Greg was in his first year of college after skipping his senior year and entering college early. You've heard part of his story. He was back and forth at home and Chris secretly had a crush on him. Chris kept her secret all through high school while Greg saw her as his little sister's friend. Things changed the summer after he graduated and came home for good. Chris had finished her first year of college and was no longer a child.

As the two began to spend time together, they fell in love. Time passed, Greg moved into an apartment and Chris was living at our house. One evening Chris came to tell me that she was going to go over to Greg's but she was not coming home that night. I said to both of them, "You know how we feel about this, but it is not our business." Greg vehemently and verbally agreed it was not our business.

A few months later, Chris again sat down with me and told me that she and Greg were going to move in together. I was not happy about it, as she knew I would not be, but all I did was entreat her to please be careful about getting pregnant.

What happened next appeared to many of my friends to be quite "crazy." I helped Greg and Chris furnish their apartment. I gave them things we didn't need and we checked out garage sales. My heart could do nothing less than to keep loving and accepting my young adults. Helping them did not mean that I condoned their behavior. There was no question in their minds that I disagreed, but there was also no question that I loved them. I had to practice what I'd preached on an even deeper level than ever before. Some friends disagreed with my stand to love and accept regardless of behavior, and I received a lot of flak.

A few months went by and I could see that Chris was a very unhappy young woman. In fact she was miserable. Finally one day she came to tell me that she was no longer going to live with Greg because God had told her to move out. After much pain from realizing that if she obeyed God, she would very likely lose this young man whom she had dreamed of having for so long. Chris moved back home with her mother.

Greg was furious—but in a day or two he realized what he was losing. Together they made an appointment with Scott (the man who had helped us with Jodi) and went to talk to him about what they should do. With Scott's help they dealt with God and each other, receiving and giving forgiveness. Scott led them in a prayer where God gave them a beautiful picture of Him cutting the soul ties they had formed. God took the ends of the "strings" and held them in His hand and told Greg and Chris that on their wedding night He would restore the connection as He intends it to be when done properly in marriage. With God's grace, Greg and Chris remained pure until their marriage a year later, when God kept all His promises.

Both Sides

I tell these stories here to bring hope to those of us whose teens or young adults appear to be straying from the fold. I think the stories sum up what I tried to say in the chapter about wayward teens and how important it is to accept them even if their behavior is not so great. By this time in my journey, I'd had to rely on God to bring me through just about everything I'd learned about teens. I had to trust that letting someone go their own path was the best thing to do even if it tore out my heart. I had to hold on to God working things out in His way and time. Most of all I did not want to lose the relationships and that reality is my reward to this day. Of course, retrospect makes it easier to see that God was faithful, but let's not let that keep us from hope and reliance on Him.

So, some might be wondering why there are no juicy stories about my other two. All I can say is that the older two did not stray from God as they went through their teens. What they had with God was real and viable to them from a very young age. There are probably several other reasons, one of which had to do with our church situations being different with each pair of teens as they came along. But what I usually tell others is this, "If I had only had the first two, you would not like me very much, because I would be full of pride that I had done such a great job." There is nothing like a wayward teen to keep one humble.

Today I am glad that I have been on both sides and can relate with hope to other parents. The younger two were more "normal" in a lot of ways and God used the hard things I went through with them to teach me deeper trust and dependence on Him. I thank God every day for my wonderful children and for the path that each trekked through the years and how God used each one's journey to make them who they are today. Knowing that God was there in each one's trek is part of seeing them as individuals and loving them the way they are. I would not change anything about them. Their individuality makes each one a unique, obedient, loving servant of God and I am grateful to God every day for His grace and faithfulness to all of us.

Share Our Power

Sharing power with teens is something I learned from Dr. Wilder. He writes extensively about power in his book, *The Red Dragon Cast Down*.[29] He says that children notice in their family who has the power, how it is used, and what the results are of having power. They notice that the one with power does not suffer (feel pain). This is usually Dad. If power is not shared properly, children learn to believe, *if I have power, I will not have pain*. This creates a desire to have power in order to control, to avoid pain, to get their way, and to overpower others in order to feel powerful. The result is a person filled with fear and anger. (pp. 169, 176)

Dr. Wilder continues, "Providing your children with power and teaching them how to use it well, is a major form of Satan-proofing your children. Powerful children can do hard things. Building powerful love bonds is how we build powerful children" (p. 168). We parents can use three very good questions to evaluate our use of power and what we are communicating to our children about power: "What kind of power did our dad have? What got him to use it? And what induced him to share his power?" Parents must share their power lovingly if they want their children to grow to healthy adults. (p. 133, 134)

So comes the obvious question—how do parents share their power? Dr. Wilder gives a few suggestions: Help teens achieve their goals. Support their dreams when possible. Teach them to think wisely, to solve problems on their own, and to plan things. Give them some power over their environment—their room, appropriate choices, their personal style. Help them learn to live with limitations. Make love bonds and not fear bonds. The strength of love bonds not only builds strength to do hard things, love bonds affect how people hear the Gospel. They are more

---

[29] *Red Dragon Cast Down*, E. John Wilder, PhD., Chosen Books, Grand Rapid, MI, 1999

likely to want to know Jesus when they see that our love for the Lord is greater than our fear. (pp. 172, 155)

It seems to me that we also share power with our teens when we stay relational and act like ourselves when upset. Angry power is not blasted onto the teen. And again when we do fail, we seek forgiveness. We send a strong message about sharing power when we can allow the teen to speak the truth in love *to us* when needed. I had such an opportunity with my oldest son, Jim, when he was about eleven years old.

Around this time, Jim (11) and I both were learning to walk in the Spirit and have an intimate relationship with Jesus. I wanted Jesus to change me in any way He wanted to. And I had my list ready. At the top of my list was—Stop yelling at my kids. So one day I sat down with Jim and we made a pact. We would help each other stop losing our tempers. If he heard me yell, he would scratch the top of his head. If I heard him yell, I would scratch the top of my head. No one else had to know what was going on. We would remind one another.

I want to say, it did not take very long before I stopped yelling and growling at my kids. It was wonderful! It was great! It was easy, because I had an instant, non-condemning reminder. The blessing from sharing power with my son was mostly mine, though he benefited as well.

Here is a story from Lisa that demonstrates how she shares her power when it's her teen that's upset with her.

Shared Power

I have been changing the way I respond when my kids get defensive with me. Instead of responding by giving consequences for their anger, I have been viewing their defensiveness as a red flag indicating I have just potentially hurt them in some way. Recently, my oldest son and I were enjoying connecting and relating with one another. A while later we got into a conflict and he lashed out at me. I responded by saying, "Jason, I must have just done something to make you feel angry or hurt. Do you know what that was? It is a blind spot for me and I want to apologize so we can get back to being close again." He told me and I quickly apologized saying I was wrong. He immediately got soft again and we returned to being close again.

Wow! What a great way to calm a potentially intense situation. Thank you, Lisa for that story.

Grace Versus Legalism

And what if we do "everything right" within our power and strive to follow God while rearing our children and the results in our teen's life are not what we'd hoped? When that is the case, we have to stay away from toxic shame and condemnation when we think about or talk with our teen about disappointments or failures. We don't go to condemnation even when we talk *about* him or her to others.

It's important to avoid using any kind of verbal threats concerning God and how He may be evaluating behavior. Legalistic threats do not work or help. Legalistic threats paint a distorted view of God and create very detrimental results to a teen's heart. When led by God, we do speak to behavior, but we speak to it in love with Relational Circuits on without condemning the teen. Love and acceptance without condoning the behavior, will go much further in keeping that relationship more important than the problem. There will be failures and disappointments along the way by both teens and parents. Regardless of the messes, we don't condemn the teen or ourselves. There is no place anywhere for any kind of condemnation.

Think about Deuteronomy 6:7: "And you shall teach these words I commanded diligently to your sons and talk of them when you sit in our house and when you walk by the way and when you lie down and when you rise up." The verse is not telling us to bash our children over the head with God's wrath, but rather to speak of His love and acceptance. And when speaking of His ways to live, to speak without condemnation, to speak about why it's better to follow God's ways—and then leave the young person in God's hands.

SUMMARY

As we come to the end of our time here, I want to remind us that, "More is caught than taught." It is vital that we parents grow in maturity, recover from our wounds, and move forward in faith so as to be the best models possible.

Joy is the way we thrive best, and I am thankful that building joy is such a rewarding activity that benefits us all, making it easier for us to thrive. As we spread joy smiles and come alongside of one another, we will find the strength to suffer well. Synchronizing with our young people will put us on the same page, build trust and understanding, and enable us to reconnect after conflict. In addition, we must share the load of parenting, the pain of recovery, and the tasks for maturity with others in authentic, joy-filled relationships.

If we desire a strong healthy family filled with mature people, we will have to walk on our "knees" some of the time, ask for help, and set aside pride that will cause us to stumble. None of us can parent perfectly and no teen will turn out without a flaw. We wouldn't need Jesus if we could be perfect. So wherever we are in our journey, when we find ourselves in a mess, don't dismay—find God in the mess—He *is* there and deeply desires to meet us where we are.

We can surround ourselves with help from others who have gone before us. We cannot parent alone. Even if we feel alone, we remember God is there. I look back on what I did not know and I grieve. I look back on God's grace in spite of what I didn't know and I gratefully thank Him. I look back and thank my children for their forgiveness and love. Because I've lived through it all, I want to encourage all readers to hold on to the fact that God's grace and faithfulness are greater than our limitations and failures. He is not surprised by anything in our lives. He has made a way for us to make it—He's here—and He truly desires that we thrive.

AFTERWORD: TREY'S TESTIMONY

Shawnda Myers has shared many hopeful stories in these pages of how changing her parenting impacted her family. Learning how to synchronize with others, how to stay relational and act like herself, and that joy means we are glad to be together no matter what, Shawnda began to parent differently.

At this writing it has been four years, and I asked her son Trey, now 20, if he would share with us his side of the story. What follows is his perspective of how things changed in their family.

Having a living example of how the skills in this book can change your relationships will give you hope. Matching Shawnda's stories in the book with Trey's comments will make you smile. Thank you, Trey, for your time and your encouragement to all who read this book.

Before

Before my mom (Shawnda) started going to Barbara's group and learned about relational joy, synchronizing, and maturity, our house was full of conflict, arguing, and fighting about anything and everything. It was pretty rough my last few years of high school. I was homeschooled and I felt controlled. Everything was decided for me and I felt restricted. My mom was always asking me to do something, to produce something, and there were all kinds of expectations. It was "her way or the highway."

I was a bit like that myself and I could be stubborn and combative. My dad and I are very alike—almost the same kind of person. We are both combative, and don't find it easy to back down, so things used to escalate when there was conflict. With both parents, I often felt defensive and on guard.

Sometimes I felt like a servant in the house. It felt like Mom was always talking, nagging, and asking lots of questions, and I didn't like to be interrupted. Sometimes there was so much conflict, Mom would leave.

There was a lot of door slamming. I wanted to get out of the house as soon as I could find a way. Now four years later, I am glad to be living there.

How Mom and I Changed

Mom was in Barbara's group for about six months before I started noticing that something was different. The first thing I noticed was that Mom quit yelling up the stairs to me when she wanted to talk to me. (*See Shawnda's story on page 26.*) When she started coming to my room to ask me if I had a second, I was still a little combative. Even when she came to find me, she still talked too much and bombarded me with too many questions. Slowly that diminished, and I noticed she was using less words. She was learning to "synchronize" and notice my energy level and read my non-verbal cues. It made me want to make time to listen.

One day when Mom came to my room to ask me to do something for Dad, who was out of town, she read my non-verbal expression because she said at the end, "It's OK for you to say 'No'." (*See story on page 105.*) I was shocked. I couldn't believe what I was hearing. I thought to myself, "What's going on here? Well in that case…." So I said, "No."

Sometimes after that I would say no, but slowly I began to do more on my own, especially if I could do it in my time. I might say no to loading the dishwasher, but then add, "I will do it later."

Mom really changed her attitude and requests about chores. When she started asking me if I would do my part, instead of saying she needed me to help, it made a huge difference. . (*See story on page 70.*) I felt like I was part of the household, instead of a slave who had to do chores every Saturday. It felt more like I belonged. She didn't tell me what my part was, how much I had to do, or criticize how I did it. Mom began to look at me differently, as she realized I had a life, I had plans and things to do, and I was a person in my own right. It really helped that I knew I was free to say no. It's not the same to ask, if the other person can't say no. Now I don't have to be on guard and afraid of conflict. The more my parents let go of me, the more I have come back on my own to do what I need to do.

This is my favorite story. When I decided to buy my first truck, Mom told me she did not want it to be big and loud. At that time I was still a little combative, so I came home with the loudest, biggest truck there was. Later, Mom told me that trucks had been a trauma for her in the past. (*See story on page 20.*) When she told me this I felt compassion for her. Then she said she was OK because Jesus had healed the trauma. I also like hearing her story of synchronizing with me when I talked on and on about the truck, and she listened and thought good thoughts towards me that showed up on her face. (*See story on pages 16 and 73.*)

Mom's cigar story shows how much she changed in these years. (*See story on page 71.*) I don't think I intended to tell her I was smoking cigars, but there it was on the counter when she walked into the kitchen. I realized that I better explain. Her reaction was the total opposite of what she would have done and said, before she learned these relational skills. She would have given me a lecture, maybe grounded me, and for sure criticized and judged me.

Instead she asked Jesus about it later and came back the next day to say that Jesus had told her to tell me to smoke cigars with Him. I laughed and agreed to do that. I received it. Her old reactions would have made me want to go out and smoke lots of cigars, maybe some cigarettes, and dip at the same time. Instead I hardly smoked many cigars, and still only smoke one or two a year. I laugh and smoke with Jesus.

I learned a lot about grace from the changes in Mom. She responded differently, even if I did something wrong. She modeled and taught me how to be more relational. I learned to pick up on my non-verbal cues. She had to be the emotionally mature one and stay glad to be with me no matter what. Even if we both were wrong, we stayed glad to be together. Then the conflict did not escalate. After a conflict, she modeled how to return to joy and be glad to be together again. At first, I was still combative and immature. Mom stayed calm most of the time, and I began to see that it was not always about conflict, but actually things that had to be done.

Changes with Dad

Dad and I are not as combative as we used to be. Dad's been learning these skills, too. He demands less and asks more. Sometimes he just asks if I'm okay. We don't escalate into intense emotions like we used to.

Just recently an incident happened that is a good story to share. Dad had been on the phone for a while with a bad situation at work. He started telling me that my room was dirty and needed cleaning. (I am unusually neat for a young adult.) This was out of the blue, and I was pre-occupied so I wasn't really listening. I began to hear what he was saying, and noticed his grumpy mood, which is not like him. So I calmly said, "Now is not the time to talk about this." He started back with me about my room, and I said again, "My room is not real dirty, but regardless, this is not the time to talk about it." Mom was there and looking a little frightened about what might happen next as I spoke a boundary. Dad didn't say anything, but I could see the gears turning. He walked away. Later, I went to work on cleaning my room.

The next day at dinner, right before I was supposed to share with Barbara's group, Dad said to me, "You should tell this story tonight. It's a cool story." That shows me how much he has changed, too.

Staying relational, noticing someone has their Relational Circuits off, and that they are not acting like themselves helps me stay calm and not react so that things escalate. Staying calm and relational even helps situations deescalate.

Other Changes in Me

As I started to notice differences in my mom's responses, at first it was alien. I realized it was more peaceful, not perfect—just cool and more peaceful.

I can look back and see big changes in how I am relating to my current girlfriend versus my previous girlfriend. I did not have good relational skills, or enough emotional maturity, to help my first girlfriend through her problems. I basically rescued her and felt her feelings for her. That was a lot of hard work to feel hers and mine, too. Now my girlfriend and I stay glad to be together when things are rough or painful, but we remind each other not to rescue or feel the other's feelings. Now I validate her feelings and show non-verbally that I care, that I understand, and I help her get through the feelings.

I have learned to separate personhood from behavior when I look at people. People are not what they do. Just because I don't do my laundry every week does not mean I'm lazy. It helps me with people outside my home, especially at work. They might not be my friends, but I can still be glad to be with them, without feeding into their drama and lies. I don't feel their feelings for them.

I had a very difficult relationship at work, and I handled it with calmness and maturity. If my mom and I had not changed, I might have handled the situation with violence, especially if the difficult person had harassed someone else. In this particular situation, I had to stay away from the person. He was not safe and I was not glad to be with him—and that was okay.

Recently we had two people living with us for a few weeks, both of whom were going through very difficult times. It was interesting to note how we still felt peaceful in our home in spite of the painful situations. We had such a good reserve of joy built up that there was no judging and no conflict. We were just glad to be together. I believe it helped the two people feel more stable. It was not a happy time, but it was a joyful time because we were glad to be together.

Not a lot gets me going any more. Through everything I have come out with an overwhelming sense of self-security of who I am and who we are as a family. This helps me deal with others and their insecurities. I don't have to prove myself. My family is a safe community and I can express myself without fear of judgment or conditions. I am very thankful that my mom learned to be relational.

Trey

APPENDIX

Hand Exercise for Overwhelm Cues[30]

Part of good relating is the ability to recognize non-verbal cues that tell us when we or others are getting overwhelmed. This is a right brain skill that can be learned with practice. Here are some ways to practice:

Break into pairs. Each will take a turn doing this. Sit facing each other about eighteen inches apart, arms length from each other's face. There will be two reasons for the exercise. 1) Realizing when I need to say, "Stop," if someone is overwhelming or pushing me. 2) Watching the other person's face, eyes, body to realize when I am overwhelming them.

Begin with Number 1: Person A hold your open hand up by your own shoulder and slowly move it towards Person B's face. They should notice how their body feels and say stop when your hand gets within their comfortable range. They can think about someone they are not comfortable with if needed. You can do this more than once and then switch. Both have a turn and discuss how it felt.

Number 2: Person A moves the hand but this time watches closely for *non-verbal* cues as to when to stop their hand, without being told, noticing when the other wants it to stop. Person B can think of someone they are not comfortable with. Person B can then say if Person A "guessed" when to stop correctly. Discuss. You can do more than once. Reverse people. Discuss how it felt.

---

[30] See *Transforming Fellowship* for more exercises. Chris M. Coursey, joystartshere.com

Immanuel Prayer for Healing

There is not time here to explain all about Immanuel Prayer. The gist is that Jesus takes us back to an unresolved painful memory and shows us that we were not alone—He was with us. During a session Jesus can also show us what the painful incident caused us to believe wrongly about ourselves. He then shows us what is true from His perspective.

Often we need a facilitator to help us with the healing prayer, but it is possible to do by oneself. Immanuel prayer will do more to change one's life that just about anything else. Please check out the *Share Immanuel* booklet from lifemodelworks.org. Check out Dr. Karl Lehman's books, *Outsmarting Yourself* and *The Immanuel Approach* at kclehman.com. Check out *Joyful Journey* as well for more information on listening prayer that can be done by oneself.

Two Voices

By Barbara Moon

The following list is a simple way to determine if you are hearing the enemy's voice or God's voice. With practice you can improve your ability to trust that you are "hearing" God in your Immanuel moments.

SATAN'S VOICE	GOD'S VOICE
Condemns	Convicts
Performance-Based Acceptance	Jesus-Based Acceptance
Lies	Truth
Loud	Soft (1 Kings 19:11-12)
Selfish	Unconditional love
Discouraging	Encouraging
Worry, Doubts	Trust Me
Fear	Faith and Love
Presses Down	Lifts up
Death Giving	Life Giving
Dark	Light
Sin Conscious	Righteousness Conscious

RECOMMENDED READING AND RESOURCES

(All books on amazon.com)

Book from Life Model Works/joystartshere.com

RARE Leadership, Marcus Warner and E. John Wilder, PhD., Moody Publishers, Chicago, 2016, joystartshere.com and deeperwalkinternational.org

Transforming Fellowship, Chris M. Coursey, Shepherd's House, 2016, joystartshere.com

Share Immanuel, E. John Wilder and Chris M. Coursey, 2010, joystartshere.com

Joyful Journey, Wilder, Kang, Loppnow, Loppnow, 2015, joystartshere.com

Joy Starts Here, Wilder, Khouri, Coursey, Sutton, 2014, joystartshere.com

Living with Men, Wilder, 2004, Shepherd's House, lifemodelworks.org

Living from the Heart Jesus Gave You, Friesen, Wilder, et. al., 2013, Shepherd's House, lifemodelworks.org

Books from Barbaramoonbooks.com or amazon.com

Joy-Filled Relationships, Barbara Moon, 2012, barbaramoonbooks.com, amazon.com

Handbook to Joy-Filled Parenting, Barbara Moon, 2007, barbaramoonbooks.com, amazon.com

Living Lessons on Intimacy with Christ, Barbara Moon, 2013, barbaramoonbooks.com, amazon.com

Re-Framing Your Hurts: Why You Don't Have to Fear Emotional Pain, Barbara Moon, 2015, barbaramoonbooks.com/amazon.com

Books from kclehman.com

Outsmarting Yourself, Karl Lehman, M. D., 2011, kclehman.com

The Immanuel Approach for Emotional Healing, Dr. Karl Lehman, 2016, kclehman.com

Book from openbench.com/amazon.com

The Bridges of Chara, Denisia Christine Huttula, openbench.com

Made in the USA
Columbia, SC
15 July 2024